MW00943328

Seeking Human Kindness

A collection of inspirational & true short stories

Inspired by true stories.
Images were given by permission of the author or
are copyright free.

ISBN-13: 978-1500391393
ISBN-10: 1500391395

First paperback edition published in 2014.
Publisher: Reading Harbor, Lansdale, P.A.

For those who believe
in the beauty of their dreams

"*Kind hearts are the gardens,*
Kind thoughts are the roots,
Kind words are the blossoms,
Kind deeds are the fruits."

~ 19th century school book rhyme

Table of Contents

Preface

One spring day, I woke up with sunlight shining on my face, and a warm idea. I wanted to write a book, one that was funny, quirky, inspiring and real. It would make people feel joy inside. When people read it, they would be reminded of that which is good in the world. It would make their day shine brighter, and their footsteps lighter.

Of course, I knew I couldn't write a book like this alone. That would require talent more than I possess, so I recruited the help of family and friends to scan the globe for the best voices we could find from around the world.

The stories we collected have a theme in common: these tales describe random acts of kindness, and the impact such good deeds had on both the giver and the recipients.

What we found surprised us, not because we didn't believe people could be good, but because it's now abundantly clear that even small acts can make such a big difference to so many. Many people who have written the stories here have gone through incredible hardships – suffering from poverty, homelessness, AIDS, freak accidents, and even what looked like it would be inevitable death.

What amazed us was how many of those who endured these pains were able to survive and thrive through the kindness and support of others, who were sometimes even strangers.

We found acts of incredible courage, where women isolated in their society were able to overcome enormous cultural and socioeconomic barriers. Along the way, they literally changed the lives of others around them through education and by their leadership example.

Strangers went out of their way to help someone else in need on a whim and discovered they had helped those when they needed it most. Oftentimes, good deeds paid the strangers back ten-thousand fold. They were responsible for changing the course of a life or even more than one live. In the process, they often found their own lives changed.

Some people had simply challenged themselves to make the world a better place. They consciously decided to do some random act of kindness because they had been inspired to do better or be better. We saw the skepticism with which their good behavior was met. In this jaded world, many skeptics roam – ready to drag others down. We saw the effects kindness had on their lives and others whom they touched when their incredulity turned into belief. Their good behavior became contagious!

Our stories come from every populated continent in the world. They come from writers of all ages, backgrounds, races, countries, and life experiences. We were able to winnow our stories down to fifty of our very favorites.

We would like to say that this collection is only a small sample and testament to the greatness of mankind. People endure many difficulties. We suffer a lot. Life is random; it can throw you curveballs when you least expect it. But, together we grow. When we help each other we achieve magnitudes beyond what we can accomplish on our own.

A lot of books we read are great because they leave us with a lasting impression. This book, a compilation of some of the most amazing stories we gathered, aims high. Our tales come from places as far-ranging as Ethiopia, Mexico, Guyana, Spain, France, China, and Taiwan, to the United States. We want to inspire you, make you feel good, and help you realize the impact that you can have.

Hopefully, this collection will be a ray of sunshine to the start of your day, the same as it was for us. We hope you like it as much as we do!

- Grace Chen

Grace Y Chen

Founder of Reading Harbor

A Little Bit of Help
Vanessa Pasco Lobrigas, Philippines

In mid-May, I saw a post on social media, which caught my eye. It was a short message about a hungry old man. He was clutching a small bottle of water while approaching a small food stall just beside a highway in Davao City. His picture was also posted.

The woman who posted it related that this old man looked very tired and hungry from walking. Eventually, he had to rest in one of the chairs at the food stall. The stall operator casually asked the old man why he looked so tired. He smiled a little bit and said that it was because it was so hot. His stomach growled. Upon pressing him, she discovered he'd run out of money to buy food. Out of compassion, the woman offered him cold water. Seeing how eagerly he drank it, she bought him a cup of rice and some fried fish and veggies to eat, too.

She said that it broke her heart looking at the old man trying to catch his breath and trying to rest himself as if nothing were the matter. It was already noon and the weather in the Philippines is so hot at that hour...

After eating, the woman asked the old man his name and asked, again, the reason he looked so tired and hungry. Then, she said in her post, "What breaks my heart most is finding out the reason why he was out under the sun just wandering like there's no place to go. The old man finally told me that it's been three days since he's been in the city looking for his daughters. He hasn't seen them for almost ten years already…"

He said, "I'm from Mati," a province in the Philippines about 4-5 hours away by foot. "I'm looking for my two daughters to tell them that their mother passed away last week. We haven't had any means of communication for almost ten years now and I'm looking for them because I have no place to go anymore, I am old and have no relatives left in our province."

The old man's tears fell while telling his story. The woman also cried and didn't know what to do to help the man, wishing she could do more. Then, suddenly she realized she was holding her phone and asked him his daughters' names as well as his name. She took a photo of him and posted it on the social media, telling her friends the story of the man's journey and the purpose of her post. She asked her social media friends to share her post to everyone they knew because – maybe, just maybe, one of his daughters or relatives living in the city, or their acquaintances – would see it and find a way to help the old man look.

After a week, there was a reply from one of the daughters saying it was her father. Knowing that he was just somewhere downtown trying to survive and looking for them made her worried; she'd had no idea what had happened to him. The post had helped reconnect them.

Of course, it was both fortune and chance that brought the old man and the inquisitive woman together. It was smart for the woman to find a way to help an old poor man find his daughters. Social media was never used better. It's odd, but a little bit of help sometimes leads to big results.

About the Author:
Vanessa Pasco Lobrigas has been a creative writer for five years. She writes theater scripts and stories for school plays in the Philippines.

Figure 1. Newspaper Photograph. Public domain image.

A Priceless Burger

By Charles Michael Tolosa, Philippines

When I was in secondary school, I used to walk ten blocks every weekday to get to class. On the plus side, it saved us a lot of gas money and provided great scenic views. On the downside, occasionally my feet would hurt, especially when I was late to class and found myself running on pavement. Generally, though, I found my morning walks to be very refreshing. The sun would shine down and open up the universe, full of life and vitality. The weather was humid but nice, not too hot or cool. I also witnessed some pretty interesting things up close, which I probably wouldn't have noticed if I had commuted by bus.

As a kid turning twelve, I didn't pay attention to some things around me as much as I might have as an adult. For instance, I wasn't really class conscious. It did strike me odd that some people would always seem to be on the streets, their clothing tattered. They often looked tired and sleepy. But, back then, it didn't really make sense to me why they would be out there.

Often, I would see one particularly elderly woman by the side of a street that I passed about a block from school. Whenever I'd turn the corner, there'd she be as reliable as the shining sun.

She had a wrinkly face and wore clothes ten times too big for her. It was odd then to see her covered with grease and dirt. Always, she would be wearing the same outfit. The slippers on her feet were a bit ripped from use. Her hair appeared as though it had not been washed in a long while. We never made eye contact. The kids would just mind their own business and head to class. Often, I'd be running because I'd woken up late. One day, though, our eyes met and I will never forget it. The look in her eyes seemed deep and empty. Something in them struck me.

Noticing my stare, she moved her body, pushing a wheelchair around to face me. How I had not noticed it before was beyond me. The chair was all battered. It made a creak as she swirled it to face me. The seat cushion, which probably had borne too much use, sagged depressingly. Some frayed stuffing poked its way out of the edges. As my widened eyes adjusted, I noticed then something even more shocking...

In the wheelchair there was also a little girl, probably around two years old, naked and covered in the same amount of grease and dirt that covered the woman's face. Her face was like mine, curious and alarmed.

My brain churned rapidly, processing this moment. The sudden realization occurred to me that this, too, was a family. Apparently, the homeless woman and her daughter took shelter in vacant lots, where there were garbage bins to rummage food from. A bit of plastic wrap from leftover sandwiches was stuck to the wheelchair, the crumbs licked clean from it. The family was bringing their "mobile home" where both of them could never fit in.

As I grew older and more mature, I started to pay more attention to my surroundings and the people around me. My parents instructed me not to talk to strangers, so my contact with the older lady and her daughter was limited to my passing observations. But, from the many instances that I saw them in the street, I can definitively say she was a loving mother. Sometimes, I would see her wiping her daughter's face with such tender caresses. Sometimes, she would carry her baby in her arms and run her fingers through her daughter's hair and down to her back. Another time, the little girl playfully ran around in circles; her mother would pick her up lovingly and tickle her. Most of the time, I'd see her walking under the heat of the sun while pushing her daughter in the shade under the buildings in that battered wheelchair, pushing the wind past them as a makeshift cooling system.

One time, I was having a really bad day. The water in our faucet was running pretty slow so I had to bathe longer than usual. I feared I was going to be late for school, again. When I went downstairs, the food prepared for breakfast was mushy and soggy. So, I did not eat it.

Cranky, I left the house with a dark cloud over my mind. As was my usual habit, I quickly walked to school to calm myself. On my way, I decided to stop by a small burger restaurant to grab something to eat before I got to school.

After walking a few blocks, I saw the woman and her daughter in a vacant lot, rummaging through an array of garbage bins.

Upon seeing them, I felt incredible guilt and shame. I wondered how someone who was deprived of all the "pleasures" in the world could have so much love in her heart, a love manifested in the way she cared for her child. My heart sank. I felt like a pretty big jerk. My worries seemed minimal, unworthy of the universe's attention. It seemed to me that I complained and ranted a lot about things that weren't a big deal. A lump formed in my throat. I resolved to try to make it right.

That realization inspired me to do something. I wasn't exactly sure what to do but I had to try something. So, despite my parents' concern, I approached them. I had observed them for a while; we sort of knew each other. To be honest, I wasn't really sure what I was going to say, but I just went for it.

As I came near, she turned and looked at me. Then, without saying anything, I thrust out to her the plastic bag that contained the burger I had just bought. My eyes lifted for an instant and met hers. To my surprise, her eyes were bright and shining. She flashed a huge smile, which revealed a prominent gap in her front teeth. Despite the physical imperfection, it was one of the most beautiful smiles I have ever seen. To this day, I remember how it made me feel, so wonderful and warm inside. She thanked me. Suddenly feeling very bashful, I responded with a small nod and quickly walked away. I knew that she was really grateful for what I did, but to be honest, they were the ones who did something great for me.

Although I looked for them, I didn't see them again. Having grown up now, I will never forget them and that moment we shared. To this day, I remember that time in my life. Whenever something bad happens or times get rough, whenever I am not appreciative enough for the fortunes I've had, I think back to how much it really takes to be happy. I try not to complain so much anymore.

About the Author:
Charles Michael Tolosa earned his B.A. in Mass Communications from Ateneo de Davao University. He has a deep passion for literature, filmmaking, music, and writing. He is currently a book editor in the Philippines.

Figure 2. "Living from Waste." Manila, Philippines. Courtesy of Getty Images.

A Seemingly Insignificant Act
By David Fribbins, United Kingdom

Note: Names have been changed to protect the identities of those involved.

Bleep, bleep, bleep, bleep, bleep…

Rolling over, Sarah raised her arm out of the duvet and switched off her six a.m. alarm with a deft swipe of her wrist. Usually she wouldn't be up this early but this month was different; this month was *important.*

Drudgingly, she willed herself out of bed, slid into her slippers and, by sheer effort, made her way down each step to the kitchen… It wasn't long before the smell of coffee had sharpened her senses and fought back the tide of early morning lethargy.

Cup in hand, she sat newly empowered at the breakfast table and began sifting through her emails, as she had often of late. Myriad offers, including the usual advertisements, Facebook notifications, and missives from recently deposed kings of Nigeria flooded her inbox – but that wasn't on this morning's agenda. Sarah clicked rapidly through until she found what she was looking for.

At 6:05 a.m., an email was delivered from *40acts.** The same emails had been arriving for just over a week now. Straight into the inboxes of Sarah and the 45,000 others who had heeded the call to challenge, a mission to give unto others during Lent.

"One green thing:" – today's act is to change something simple, like switching from plastic bags to reusable ones, or walking to work a few days a week instead of using the car.

"Ughhh," Sarah groaned aloud. She needed to go into town later that day to do some shopping, as her cupboards were almost bare of Arabica beans and now she wasn't going to be driving. Sometimes it was hard to keep going, but she was committed and only a week in.

As time is wont to do, hours passed by. Six o'clock had turned into morning and morning into afternoon, by which time Sarah had managed to magically get clothed, fed somehow, and was just about ready to go do her good deed of the day.

After one final swig of coffee, she dropped her car keys on the side table, locked the door, and began the walk into town. To her surprise, it was a lovely day. The sun was bright and the skies were clear. Her mood greatly improved as Mother Nature cheered her on.

If anything were amiss, the only negative thing to be said about walking that day was that every now and again an unwanted gust of wind would rear its ugly head in jest, whipping and splaying Sarah's hair all over her face. At this obnoxiousness, Sarah dug her hands deep into her pockets and was pleasantly relieved to find a treasured hair band.

Then something interesting happened.

Another gust of wind roared through the street carrying with it a small piece of paper. It isn't uncommon to find paper on streets – to be fair it is probably safe to go one step further and say that streets often have scrap pieces of paper on them – at least in London anyway. Normally, Sarah wouldn't notice, but today she was being "green."

Picking up the piece of paper, she looked around to find a rubbish bin. A few hundred meters over and she would have completed her mission for that day twice. As she began to walk towards the bin, something struck her. She looked down at the scuffled and folded paper. Barely perceptible, nearly illegible giant block letters spelled out the faint name *Amy* across the sheet. Without thinking, Sarah put the paper into her empty pocket and walked straight past the bin.

En route to the town, there is a local primary school filled with loud, bubbly and excitable children, especially at the end of the day. The mothers (and a few fathers) had begun to congregate and the decibels had been steadily rising, from silent to nattering to "I can't hear what you are saying but I'll nod anyway." Today, however, there was another sound amongst the usually mirthful crowd.

Unbeknownst to Sarah, an inconsolable child, age three, earlier that day had written her name on a piece of paper for the first time in her life…

For those who have seen it, an inconsolable child is hard not to notice. Generally, adults have an instinct to protect little ones and try to comfort them, especially if tears are flowing profusely from a little cherub face. As Sarah tried to pilot her way across the street, she was struck by the scene of a positively distraught angelic little creature. Instinctively, wanting to help, she wished she could have done something. The mother seemed to pat the child and look frightfully worried. "You can write another one."

Feeling the crumpled paper in her pocket, Sarah suddenly had an audacious thought. Plucking up the courage, Sarah asked if the little girl's name was Amy. Confused and surprised, the mother tentatively responded with a bewildered "Yes." On seeing the note, the little girl's face lit up with joy.

Even now, having thought through that day, Sarah can't offer a rationale for why she walked past the bin – she says that she just knew that the name on the paper was important.

This seemingly insignificant and easily passed-by act probably made a big impact for Amy that day, but was far more profound and longer lasting for Sarah. Signing up for

40acts, making the decision to walk instead of drive, picking up a piece of paper, and all of the other seemingly insignificant choices that were made, all contributed to the overwhelming joy of a child.

To this day, Sarah sometimes muses to herself about how a simple, little piece of paper could mean so much to two people. Little things can, and often do, make a big difference.

*40acts (www.40acts.org.uk) is an online generosity campaign running throughout Lent. Its purpose is to encourage and inspire people to give away rather than just give up.

About the Author:
David Fribbins is a young man from Britain with a love for words and other creative... stuff. He is a writer whose library of work is an ever growing coliseum of unfinished stories and yet-to-be-switched-on light bulbs. While working on his own projects, he is always on the lookout for new inspiration and new opportunities to use his skills and help others.

A Simple Gesture

By Chelsea Resnick, North Carolina, USA

Striding alongside my soon-to-be husband, Daniel, and my teenage sister, Rose, we huddled deeper into our coats and steeled ourselves against the drizzle as we entered Times Square.

"Maybe the rain will keep the crowds away," said Daniel, ever the optimist.

Despite the chills shimmying up my arms, I cracked a smile. The morning was a culmination of childhood dreams. During my Midwestern youth, I'd shuffled into the living room on many a Thanksgiving morning. With pajamas hanging like curtains from my small frame, I'd nestled into the couch to watch the annual Macy's Thanksgiving Day Parade. In the nearby kitchen, my parents would be brining the turkey and chopping stuffing fixings.

Such grade school memories had long afforded the parade a sentimental luster in my thoughts. Of course, as an adult, I knew it was "only" a parade. I knew about corporate sponsors and excuses for selling kitschy NYC wares to an influx of tourists. Still, my inner six-year-old was thrilled: the balloons! the high-kicking Rockettes! the Broadway numbers performed on confetti-sprinkled streets!

My fellow travelers and I stationed ourselves at an opening along the parade route and soon discovered that on this cold, wet morning, other parade-goers were not so warmed by childhood escapism. There was the man beside us who refused to angle his umbrella so as not to gush rainwater down Daniel's right shoulder. There was the rouge-lipped woman who elbowed me aside, grousing that she was saving spots for her teenage nieces and nephews. For every cheerful person, there seemed to be another with a temper vocally soured by the crowds and weather.

Still, Rose, Daniel, and I refused to let the morning's hiccups faze us. The rain eventually abated, and when Santa Claus arrived in a flurry of blaring Christmas carols and elf balloons, the parade drew to its close. The crowds quickly dispersed. We looked down at our clothes, which had seemingly quadrupled in weight thanks to the chilled rainwater soaking them.

"Well, it's about lunchtime," Daniel said. "Should we get something to eat?" We each looked from one to the other, all thinking the same thing: We'd saved money for this trip, sure. But the price of eating out in New York City was making an impression. We'd made restaurant reservations for that evening, and the costs would quickly stack up.

"Do you guys just want to hit up a food cart?" I asked. We could see several such options from where we stood.

And so we meandered toward 45th Street, planning a quick jaunt back to the hotel where we could freshen up. When we paused in front of a pretzel stand, I sifted through my wallet.

"Three pretzels please," I told the man beneath the cart's umbrella. Expressionlessly, he ripped out three pieces of parchment paper, one for each knot of bread, and a moment later, my companions and I turned with our pretzels in hand. There was no place to lounge and eat, so, like the salmon of the Northwest, we instinctively joined the stream of people moving down the sidewalk.

Just then, Rose tipped her chin toward me, pursing her lips to speak. That was when her pretzel slipped from its parchment.

Down,

Down,

Down…it fell.

Although I saw it happen with eyes drawn wide, I didn't possess the superhero reflexes to react. The pretzel bounced on the pavement halfway between a grease puddle and two flattened wads of bubblegum. The three of us mutely stared, our shoulders falling like a round of The Wave at a baseball game.

With a sigh, I again reached for my wallet. "We'll get you a new one," I told Rose. At least, we were only a few feet from the cart.

All around, people marched, their motions as determined as soldiers, as fluid as dancers. In the corner of one eye, I happened to notice a young man stride past. He was tall and thin, likely in his mid- to late twenties. With his navy pea coat and a vacant gaze, his appearance didn't beg for attention. In fact, he only caught my eye because he paused at the same pretzel cart to which I was about to return.

The remarkable part was how he never broke his stride. He breezed by us, pulling out his wallet. He handed the man at the cart a few dollar bills in exchange for a pretzel. Then he spun around, proffering the new pretzel to a gape-mouthed Rose. In the same motion, he pivoted back on one heel and resumed his original gait down packed Broadway. Within seconds, he'd melted into the crowd again. He never uttered so much as a word, and we could only shout dumbfounded thank-yous in his wake. We turned toward the new pretzel in Rose's grasp.

Oh, that pretzel. Its purchase was a small act, not the sort of gift that saved a life or solved any geopolitical crises. Still, the simple gesture mattered.

As Rose, Daniel, and I strolled back to our hotel room, we basked in that stranger's unforeseen kindness, tucking its memory into our hearts for the long-term. What a nice reminder we received on that gazpacho-cold morning – that even amid spectacle and fanfare, life is so often about the everyday ways that we treat one another.

About the Author:
Chelsea Resnick is a Texas-born, Kansas-bred writer and editor. She's worked in an array of publishing and creative capacities, including jobs as a greeting card editor, children's books editor, and copywriter. Known particularly for her children's literature, for which she writes under the name Chelsea Fogleman, she currently writes out of North Carolina where she lives with her family. Find her online at www.chelsearesnick.com.

A Simple Meal

By Beverley Bowen-Evans, Jamaica

Ariana sat slouched in the computer lab, her eyes drifting ever so often from her screen. It was hard to focus when you hadn't eaten in a while... Sometimes, she questioned her previous resolve. Why had she left the comfort of Jamaica, a loving home, to be in this foreign place – cold, friendless, hungry and tired? Her fatigued eyes travelled to the wall, which bore the shiny school placard – and she remembered, snapping herself out of a wasteful, drowsy state.

She couldn't have passed up the chance to study overseas. It would give her and her family a much needed chance. A better job when she went back meant a better life for them all. Being the oldest of three sisters, she had to set an example. Grateful that a grant had allowed her to pay her tuition in full, she reminded herself it was a blessing to live in an apartment complex just across from campus, within walking distance to school even on snowy and rainy days. Her mother – a single parent – sent enough to cover her rent and bills. She tried to focus. This was her job.

Suddenly, a loud low grumbling noise interrupted her typing. Her mind had snapped back on track, but her stomach was a different issue. It was so hard to calm it. She rummaged in her bag but found only an empty cracker wrapper. Looking around, she hoped for a water fountain. Some days ice cubes and water were enough. If she didn't eat today, then tomorrow she might have scraped up enough for the all-you-could-eat Chinese buffet, a nice treat…

Someone shuffled into the seat next to her. An older woman Ariana recognized as Karen, from her IT class, plopped down beside her. Momentarily distracted, Ariana caught a glimpse of the woman's eyes. They shined with the unmistakable moisture of tears forming.

Before she could say anything, Karen blurted out a question. "You're in my computer networking class, right?"

"Yes, I am…" Ariana answered hesitantly, confused by the stranger's approach.

"Do you understand the assignment?!?! I'm failing this course! I need help! Please!" Karen looked at Ariana with an expression mixed with panic and desperation. Unsure if she could be of help, Ariana decided to calm the woman.

"Sure, no problem… I can try. What exactly don't you understand?"

"Ummmm… EVERYTHING!!!"

Adriana's eyes widened.

From eight a.m. till late in the evening, the two women worked, not even stopping for a break. When at last the assignment was done, both women were surprised to see that outside was dark, when it had barely been sunrise when they started.

"Oh gosh, Ariana! Thank you so much for this. You really have no idea what you've done for me. Don't worry, I'll take you home. Do you like Chinese food? I know a great restaurant right around the corner. I'll pay."

Ariana's cheeks burned. She couldn't refuse something like that, not as much as she needed it. "Thanks."

"It's the least I can do."

They bundled up into their jackets and left the lab. A few hours later, Ariana entered her apartment with several take-out containers of Chinese food. This would be able to serve her for two days!

&

The next day, Ariana had barely entered her apartment after her classes when her phone rang.

"Hello?"

"Hi Ariana! Are you home?" It was Karen.

"Yes, I am." Ariana answered, a little surprised.

"Oh good. Which apartment are you in?"

"Number 41. It's on the ground floor..."

Ariana barely managed to get the words out of her mouth before Karen cut her off.

"Okay. I'm on my way around. Listen for my knock," Karen answered in a hurry.

A few minutes later, there came the knock. As Ariana opened the door, Karen's head popped up behind a huge box. Ariana's eyes widened in surprise. She helped her classmate, who was struggling to fit through the door, get in.

"Take this one," Karen said, puffing for air.

She pushed the giant box into Ariana's arms.

The unmistakable aroma of baked goods emanated from the cardboard box.

Tears started to well up in her eyes, before Ariana could say thank you.

Karen had dashed off, shouting behind her, "I have more in the car!"

Within twenty minutes the living room floor was covered with boxes of varying sizes. Its contents held a variety of food and an assortment of baked goods from the bakery Karen managed.

Ariana was in shock.

"This is just my way of saying thank you for yesterday. Don't ask 'Why food?' I really don't know myself." With a quick hug she was out the door.

Tears came flowing. Ariana could not believe her eyes and good fortune. Who would have thought that her one act of kindness could have yielded such results? And guess what? For the next three years that Ariana was in Atlanta, her cupboards and refrigerator were never empty. Karen made sure of that.

About the Author:

Beverley Bowen-Evans has been writing stories ever since she was introduced to creative writing in her eighth grade English Language class at the Immaculate Conception High School in Kingston, Jamaica. She is a storyteller who has honed her craft over the years and continues to expand her boundaries. She has written a number of plays and stories that have aired on the local radio and published in the newspaper. She is a graduate of the Mico Teachers College in Kingston where she majored in English and Spanish. She is trained to teach at the secondary level and has been doing so since 2002.

Figure 3. A simple meal can make a big difference.

A Special Watch

By Summer White, Georgia, USA

Greg almost lost his sweaty grip on the phone. He hit the pound key to replay the message, over and over and over again. His teacher sat across the desk from him, spinning his thumbs, fumbling with his pen, appraising the thick layer of dust on the ceiling fan, looking anywhere but at Greg.

He put the phone down and hid his face in his hands. His teacher, Thomas, let out a sigh. "Maybe our financial division can you help you. Maybe there's a lawyer that would take on the case for you pro bono."

"Yeah, man," Greg said with false cheerfulness, sitting upright and wiping a lone tear from the corner of his aged, gray eyes. "Thanks for that."

"Sure, sure," Thomas nodded. "I'll talk to them and let you know. Tomorrow, maybe."

The men nodded, shook hands over the desk, and Greg made a hasty exit. Walking down the sloping lawn towards the housing area, the panic set in. His third wife had never been the most prudent with their finances but how she could rack up ten thousand dollars worth of charges in his name was beyond him.

Greg was on the cusp of completing a rigorous ten-month drug addiction rehabilitation program. Greg was, for the first time in decades, sober, happy, and at peace. For the first time since he could remember, he loved waking up in the morning. He was an integral part in the program. He was a leader, and someone the other men in the program admired.

Now, after ten months of being told that God had a plan for his life, and that if he just stuck close to God, everything would fall into place, this fell in his lap. He didn't know what he'd done to deserve such a punch in the gut.

Although usually bright-eyed and in the center of conversation, Greg was quiet and busy brooding at dinner that night. He was racking his brain for ideas. He had no money. He couldn't afford a lawyer and was done asking for handouts.

By lights-out that night, he had exhausted all possible avenues of thought. He was a convicted felon with no job, no money, and no way to protect himself from the creditors. He decided to push the matter aside in order to finish his final homework assignment in the program. He pulled out his yellow legal pad and looked at the list he had started composing earlier that week of ten things that he really wanted. The assignment was to write down ten things that you really wanted in your life, to fold the paper up, put it in your pocket, and have faith that – if you stayed on the right path – success would eventually be yours.

Greg looked through his list. His sour mood made him feel that none of those things would ever come to him. A happy marriage? Becoming a successful businessman? All of a sudden these thoughts seemed laughable to him. Dejected, and with only one more slot to fill on the list to complete the assignment before he could sleep and escape from his miserable feelings, he wrote, "10. A watch."

A watch. His teacher would ask about that, no doubt. Why, in a list of seriously wonderful, amazing things worth going after, would he add a watch? Greg smiled at his own joke, his own pronouncement of how little he thought of himself, and stuffed the legal pad back under his single bed and fell into a fitful sleep.

Two days later, Greg was setting up a microphone in the cafeteria. They were having a special guest speaker that night. A world-renowned motivational speaker was preparing to drive down their lawn in his Cadillac Escalade and inject some hope into the addicts' day. Greg was not looking forward to it, but with his usual grace, he plastered a smile on his face and went about with his busy work.

Three hours later, Greg was tearing down microphones and folding up chairs. The speaker was sitting in the corner, flanked by his entourage, signing copies of his book and flashing his shiny white teeth all over the room. Greg was encouraged by what the speaker had said and hoped to get a chance to share that with him before he left.

The crowd of people surrounding him dissipated and the speaker rose, stretched, and yawned casually. Greg took this as his moment and hurried across the room. Before the man noticed that he was about to have company, his million dollar smile was taking a break and Greg noticed a grayness in his eyes and smile lines framing his entire face. He almost – just for a second – looked more like Greg than an internationally famous figure.

As soon as the speaker noticed Greg, he fixed his trademark smile back on and reached out to shake his hand.

"Sir, that was a great presentation," Greg said quickly, shaking the speaker's hand and then fumbling nervously with his pockets. "I'm almost at the end of my program here and with the week I've been having, I really needed to hear what you had to say."

Greg and the speaker exchanged pleasantries, and the man offered to sign a copy of his glossy-covered book with a giant picture of his face on it. The speaker asked what Greg's addiction was and nodded his head as if he understood. Greg wasn't disconcerted by this; he was used to people feeling the need to appear empathetic to a problem they couldn't possibly understand. The two men discovered they both had daughters about the same age, and both of them rooted for the Cowboys.

The speaker's entourage reemerged in the doorway to the cafeteria and nodded, signaling that it was time for them to leave.

Before shaking Greg's hand the speaker bit his lip for a moment. "I don't know why, but I'm really feeling led to give this to you," he said, as he reached for his wrist. "I practically have a suitcase full of watches back in my hotel room. This one is my favorite. I really want you to have it." He slipped the silver Breitling off his wrist and handed it to Greg.

Greg was not sure what to say for a moment, and he shook his head. "Sir, I don't mean to be rude, but that is a ten thousand dollar watch. I couldn't possibly."

"No, please, take it," the speaker said, continuing to hold it out to Greg. "Something tells me you need this more than I do."

Greg used that watch to pay off the credit card debt his wife had incurred in his name. Today, Greg is clean, sober, and has successfully obtained every single item and goal he wrote down on his list.

Greg has chosen not to wear a watch.

About the Author:
Summer White is a former university English department tutor. She has written in local writer's magazines in the Atlanta area.

Broken Leg vs. the Curb
By Angel Propps, Florida, USA

"Let me give you a hand."

I'm used to saying those words, not hearing them directed at me. Yet they were being directed at me and I had to swallow down tears. There I sat, like a strangely beached animal, moored on a concrete sea. My wheelchair was stuck in a crack between the street and the sidewalk and I could not get it up and over that curb. I had never felt so foolish or terrified in all my life.

How did this happen to me? That was the question rolling through my mind as I sat there trying to figure out how to get that chair up onto the curb before the stream of traffic could begin again.

Of course I *knew* how it had happened. A week before, I took my dog for a walk and upon returning home I slipped on a patch of wet grass. I fell and got a triple fracture to my ankle and a broken femur as a result. If I had been at home, I would never have gotten stuck; my beloved would have been pushing me down the street. I never would have been navigating it alone.

I was not at home right then though. I was in New York – Manhattan, to be precise – on a work-related trip, stuck in a wheelchair I had little idea of how to operate, and fear had reduced me to a puddle. I was being condensed down to a public spectacle: a larger-sized woman in a wheelchair whose wheel had gotten trapped in a cracked chunk of asphalt. The people walking past either ignored me or snickered.

If I could have run away I would have. As fast and as far as possible.

I love Manhattan. I go all the time. I love walking the streets, eating from the food carts, and going to see shows at the little Off-Broadway (or even Off-Off Broadway) theatres. I had thought, honestly, that I could make that trip despite the cumbersome and unfamiliar chair, the inability to walk and the pain in my leg and hip.

"Let me give you a hand."

I could not see her, she was behind me. Her voice was husky, low and the precise timbre of a forties-era blues singer: smoky, rich and filled with a raspy sweetness. I imagined an older, rounder woman, one who had decades of experience stamped into her face, and a few gray hairs running through her rich black tresses. Tears no longer threatened, they breached my eyelids.

"I can't get up without falling," I stuttered out. "The chair is stuck. If I could just stand up on my good leg I could get it unstuck but I can't get a good footing here."

"No worries. Hey you!" A man walking past us stopped in his tracks. "Give us a hand will you?"

"Of course." He put his phone in his pocket and approached. "I think if she leans on me and you push the chair we can get it up and over. They really should fix that mess, it's a real danger."

I had to trust two strangers, one of whom I could not even see. The man was dressed in business attire. My hands were stained with dirt from the wheels and I said so. I added, "I have no idea why I never thought to wear gloves. I am going to wreck your shirt if I touch you."

I would have to touch him if he was going to help me up. I didn't want to destroy his pastel blue and very expensive dress shirt. He shrugged, "The laundry will get it out."

They got me up and over the hump in a matter of seconds. It felt like an eternity but it was just a matter of seconds – a few heartbeats really.

"Thank you," I managed.

They both said no problem and vanished. I never saw her, by the time I managed to swivel my head around she could have been any woman walking past. His shirt was visible for a moment and then gone too.

They appeared, helped me, and vanished. They probably have no idea of just how timely their arrivals were. How they made an entire day filled with frustration and fear and internal conflict suddenly change its entire direction.

They helped me to stand and they gave me a push over a broken edge of concrete and asphalt and they gave me hope. I could do this. I would get through it, and not just the trip but the entire ordeal.

If I could make it here, if I could depend on the kindness of people who did not even know me, I could make it all the way through.

Thank you for your kindness.

Thank you for hope.

Thank you for reminding me why doing things out of simple kindness is so important.

About the Author:
Angel Propps is a writer, musician and a big believer in kindness being a river in which we should all swim.

Car Ride

By Patrice Marrero, Massachusetts, USA

The windows were open as we rode down the highway, taking in the sun that only San Diego can provide almost every day of the year. My friend and I had made the cross-country move from Massachusetts to California about two weeks prior. We were out job hunting. I had just gotten a job offer, on the spot, and we were ready to celebrate.

The six-lane freeway was pretty busy, with rush hour fast approaching. Traffic moved along, as we sped towards our new home. I sat in the passenger seat, enjoying the new freedom I felt as a twenty-year-old, living away from home and taking care of myself.

I think I saw the truck before my friend did. It was stopped in the middle of the road up ahead, and we were barreling straight towards it. I remember thinking, "I'm not wearing my seatbelt. I am going to die," as I put my arms out in front of me to brace for the impact.

The airbags exploded, feeling like a knockout punch. As they released, a cloud of white powder gusted through the car, stinging my newly formed cuts and scrapes while making it hard to breathe. We couldn't open our doors, and the truck we'd collided with drove away, and cars sped past on either side of us. We sat there, in a state of panic. My friend had gone into shock, and I couldn't move enough to wake her. I have never felt so alone, three thousand miles away from home and everyone I loved.

Suddenly, a man in uniform opened the driver-side door. He immediately took charge, checking my friend for injuries. As soon as he saw that she was unhurt, he put his arm around her, talking quietly as he led her to the median so she could sit.

There must have been a few other angels who stopped to help. As he got in the driver's side, I heard him directing others as he turned the wheel to get the car positioned out of the line of traffic.

By now, I was trying to take stock of my injuries. It felt like I had broken every bone in my face, and as I reached for visor to pull the mirror down, a deep pain in my wrist made itself known. I switched arms, throwing my right arm up with enough force to succeed. I felt relief as I only saw some cuts on my face. I had avoided breaking my nose, not to mention I was alive.

He opened my door and knelt down, with a friendly smile, and said, "I'm a Navy corpsman, do you mind if I make sure you're okay?" Gently, he checked me for wounds. The pain in my left wrist was debilitating, and I told him so. "Have you ever broken a bone?" he asked, as he looked at my right forearm, which was now shaped like a boomerang.

"No," I answered in disbelief. "That arm is not broken, this arm is," I said as I slightly moved my left arm, writhing in pain. "Okay," he said, with the most serene look on his face and a slight chuckle that was in no way demeaning and somehow comforting, letting me believe what I needed to at the time.

He continued to look me over, ensuring that I had no critical injuries. Then he took a knee, looked me in the eyes, and said, "I think your arm is broken, but you're going to be okay." With tears falling from my eyes, I somehow released the word, "Okay."

He stayed there with me, it felt as though he was holding my hand, but he could not have been. We talked about my cross-country adventure to get to California. He told me he was on his way home from work when he saw the accident. It was like we were the only two people there, as rush hour traffic flew by and emergency workers entered the scene.

I didn't want him to leave when the police officer came to get my statement. They spoke in hushed tones for a moment before my uniformed hero bent back down to say goodbye. The moment was so rushed, I didn't get to ask his name.

I watched in the mirror I had so painstakingly pulled down, as an ambulance pulled up behind us. My angel in camouflage spoke to the EMTs, and stepped aside to lean on the median. He had finished his job, caring for me when no one else was there.

I remember thinking I would be able to find him so I could thank him. I'm from a small city, where car accidents make the paper. I assumed our wreck would be part of the daily news, and he would come forward to take the honor of being a good citizen. Unfortunately, when I woke up from surgery, it was not the case. The corpsman was right, my right arm had been badly broken. I made it through with a rod in one arm, and casts on both.

I learned a few important lessons that day. The most important: to always stop. It only took one kind stranger who stopped to help get me through a shocking situation by putting my mind at ease, just being there and letting me know that I was going to live – after thinking I was going to die. He stopped as hundreds of other cars drove by, because it "wasn't their problem." Each of us will most likely end up in a situation where we need help someday. Be thankful for those who stop.

The members of our armed forces are heroes who put their lives on the line to protect us. We think of them over in the desert, fighting wars, but they are so much more than that. They are among the first ones to help when tragedy strikes at home, too, and they do so with expertise.

Most importantly, I learned to wear my seatbelt.

Patrice Marrero is a writer who lives in Massachusetts with her husband and their dog. When she's not tapping on the keyboard, she enjoys hiking with her family, kayaking and reading as many books as she can get her hands on.

Figure 4. Patrice with her family.

Chasing Down Kindness
By Sharon Fuentes, Washington, D.C., USA

My father used to have a saying that went, "After every grave tragedy, something good emerges." But no matter how hard I tried looking after hearing about the horrific events on December 14th, 2012, I just could not find any good. Twenty children and six heroic teachers lost their lives at Sandy Hook Elementary School that day. Twenty children – babies – like my own. My mind could just not wrap itself around that.

But then it happened... the "something good" emerged. All over the internet, Facebook and even Twitter hashtags saying #26ActsofKindness started popping up. Story after story appeared of generous, kind people who were reaching out and spreading love via unexpected acts of kindness; 26 acts of kindness to be exact, an act for each of the souls who were taken that dreadful day.

Flowers left on windshields of strangers' cars in a parking lot, a person paying the toll for the vehicle behind them, a cup of coffee given to the security guard at the mall who usually goes unnoticed. Random people were trying to connect with other people, all in an effort to make some sense out of a nonsensical event that should never have happened. I knew I wanted to be a part of this kindness movement. Or perhaps it was more I NEEDED to be a part.

My heart was pure, or so I thought, and my ideas were grand. I headed out to the grocery store to purchase 26 lottery tickets. Not only was I going to spread kindness, I was going to instill hope in the future, belief that things can change. I was going to literally PAY it forward! I had some silly fantasy that one of the folks whom I would randomly give a ticket to would win the jackpot and while on TV they would thank the kind stranger who made it possible. Just think of the good karma that would bring me!

I was so excited when purchasing the tickets that I had to share my plan with someone. "I'm going to put these tickets in my children's teachers' mail slots at school tomorrow and then give some to the front office workers and janitorial staff. Everyone forgets about those folks but they are so important." I rattled on, basically tooting my own horn of greatness to the cashier selling me the tickets. The woman behind the counter suddenly got a very strange look on her face. "You mean you are giving the tickets out tomorrow?" she asked, confused. "Yes," I said, "That's the plan, why?" The woman looked at me apologetically and pointed to the date on the tickets.

I had just purchased 26 Quick Pick tickets for the drawing that would happen THAT NIGHT, five hours from then to be exact! OOPS!

"Okay, plan number two," I told the cashier as I reached back into my purse for more money. "Let me have 26 Scratch Off tickets please. And here, you take these lottery tickets back and hand them to the next person who comes to buy Quick Picks for tonight and tell them that a sweet woman wanting to spread kindness and love left them for them." I added. The woman became very nervous. "Oh no! I can't do that; I could get in trouble," she said and pushed the tickets back at me. This plan was certainly not going the way I had imagined it. I took the 26 Scratchers and my 26 Quick Picks and started to walk away.

On the way out the door it hit me (an idea, not the door). Why not give the Quick Pick tickets away right here in the store to random shoppers. Happy with my new plan, I turned around and grabbed a basket – you know, so I wouldn't look like some crazy lady who was stalking people. (Which as it turned out is exactly what I ended up looking like, it seems.)

I saw a sweet-looking older woman having a hard time trying to grab a can of clam chowder off the top shelf. "Here, let me help you with that," I said in my best Girl Scout voice. "Why, thank you dear," she said and took the can from me and turned to walk away. Now was my time to really do something nice. I tapped the woman on the shoulder and said, "Excuse me, this is for you." The woman turned around startled and looked at the ticket in my hand rather skeptically. "Here, take it. It's a Quick Pick lottery ticket for tonight's drawing. I hope you win," I said, rather proud of myself. Like a proud peacock, I started to strut away.

I hadn't gotten very far when I felt a tap on my shoulder. I turned around and found the elderly lady was looking at me rather angrily. "I am not a charity case. I don't need your pity ticket," she huffed and threw the ticket back at me and walked away, rather quickly for a woman her age I might add. "Wait! I'm sorry, that was not what I meant! It's a random act of kindness!" I yelled while trying to catch up with her.

At this point, I was starting to draw some attention from the other shoppers. I should have just called it quits; a smart person would have done just that. But nope, I kept going. After all, this was not the way things were supposed to be in my delusional fantasy. So I continued after her, ranting and raving and practically tackling the poor lady, when she stopped short. I tried to catch my breath. (How was it this little woman was not huffing and puffing too?) Finally able to breathe normally, I tried to calmly explain that I was not crazy; I was just trying to do a nice thing in honor of the folks in Sandy Hook. "My goodness, you acted like I had a gun in my hand when it was only a ticket. A lottery ticket I wanted to give you!" I said frustrated, and without really thinking.

Note to self: After a horrible tragedy that involved a person with mental illness, not a good idea to chase after a stranger in a public place and then try to tell them you are not crazy, and then reference a gun, even an imaginary nonexistent gun! Let's just say I no longer shop at that grocery store after this whole incident.

But wait! I cannot end this story here. Nope, I need to show you that my dad was right. Out of every bad thing good does emerge. I went home a bit deflated but consenting to the fact that I would do my acts of kindness at my children's school. Since I had the tickets anyway, I watched the drawing that night and well… one of the tickets was a winner. Guess how much? Yup, twenty-six dollars. Talk about irony!

The next day, I took my kids to school and brought in the Scratch Off tickets, to which I had attached a note explaining their purpose, so as not to have any more misconceptions or problems. It felt great putting these tickets in the teachers' mail slots and even better when I overheard a teacher who had found it. "This made my day!" she said. Then I watched as she held the door open for another person and commented, "Here, allow me to get that for you. Only 25 more to go," she giggled, referring to the fact that she was going to do her own 26 acts of kindness. My deed was done… I could go home.

On my way out the door, a cafeteria worker stopped me. "I'm embarrassed to ask, but some of the others said that you were giving out Scratch tickets, and I thought that perhaps you forgot to give me mine? I could sure use some luck!" she said shyly. I had given out all my tickets, but I did not have the heart to tell this very deserving soul that. I could tell she was a proud woman and for her to ask, well, she must have really been down on her luck indeed. So I told her I had left them in my car and that I would be back.

I excused myself left the school and used that twenty-six dollars I had won to buy twenty-six more Scratch Off tickets. I then put them in an envelope along with a gift card for groceries (just in case the tickets were not winners) and left it for her at the front desk. I did not want to be there when she opened it because I did not want to risk making her feel uncomfortable. Besides, I no longer needed the glory for doing a good thing. I felt it in my heart.

I learned a very important lesson that day. Kindness does not require chasing folks down and doing loud grandiose gestures making sure others see you do it. Kindness is the little extra something that we do when no one is looking!

About the Author:
Sharon Fuentes is an award-winning humor columnist, parenting guru, special needs advocate, co-author of *The*

Don't Freak Out Guide to Parenting Kids with Asperger's, and firm believer in random acts of kindness. You can contact her at Sharon@sharonfuentes.com.

Figure 5. Sharon doing a social experiment on if people treat others differently depending on how they dress.

Compliments FREE – Take One if Needed!
By Sharon Fuentes, Washington, D.C., USA

Call it a moment of genius or more likely an activity I came up with to amuse my bored children on yet another snow-day off from school; whatever you call it, it was, well, for lack of a better word – awesome! Their first few snow days were fun – sleeping in, lounging around in their pajamas, playing Minecraft when they would have been doing math if they'd been at school. But by day 3, the kids were actually begging to go back, and I won't lie to you... so was I.

It's hard to get any work done when your daughter is trolling behind you, questioning every sentence you write and getting on your nerves. I had given up being creative and was instead just checking my email inbox when my ten-year-old daughter, Grace, noticed the words, "You are an awesome writer!" in the "Re:" section of one. "Click on it, Mom! Read it!" So I did. It was a random message from someone who'd read an article I'd written and taken a few moments of their time to let me know they enjoyed it. I was on cloud nine. Seeing me so excited got my daughter excited.

Perhaps it was boredom, a case of cabin fever, or maybe it was a giant dose of pure unexpected happiness that caused the next thing that happened.

"My mom is the most awesome writer in the world!" Grace shouted and started jumping around in a circle. Her delight was contagious. "That makes you the daughter of the most awesome writer so therefore you are pretty awesome yourself!" I sang back and joined her in an impromptu awesome dance. We jumped around laughing and giggling for what had to be a good five minutes.

Finally we both stopped, yet we could not help but keep smiling at one another. "Wow, you would have thought I won a Pulitzer Prize!" I said, not quite sure what about that random comment made me feel so good. "What's a Pulitzer Prize?" my daughter said, bringing me back to earth and reminding me that I really needed to get her to broaden her reading material to include something that did not have *One Direction* on its front cover.

A question lingered in my head. Can a compliment from a complete stranger really make a difference? With this in mind I told my kids to grab their hats and coats and we set off to the grocery store to conduct an experiment, and to grab some milk and bread.

The goal was that each of us was going to give an honest, sincere, unexpected compliment to at least three random people while shopping. Grace was the first to complete her mission. "Those are adorable shoes," she said, while pointing to the red flats on the woman weighing bananas. The woman beamed with pride and said, "Thank you! They're new!" Then my sweet girl went further, "Well they are really cute, you did well!" she said matter-of-fact. The woman blushed and walked away with a bounce to her step in her pretty red shoes. "That was fun! Did you see how happy she was?" Grace said excitedly. And on and on it went. We told the man behind the meat counter he had a nice smile; the boy stocking boxes of Mac n' Cheese grinned when he was complimented on how perfectly aligned his boxes were; the cashier looked as if she'd won a jackpot when told her eyes were the loveliest shade of blue! And with each compliment we offered, we all grew even more excited and happy! We left the grocery store that day feeling rather proud of ourselves for spreading a little bit more joy. Of course it was lost as soon as we got home and the kids started arguing over whose turn it was to walk the dog; but for that brief moment in time, it was wonderful.

The snow stopped and the kids finally went back to school. During the day, the phone rang. When I saw the school's number on the caller ID my heart stopped. Who was sick, what did they forget, was someone in trouble? To my surprise, it was Grace's teacher, calling to tell me about something GOOD Grace had done. Grace had made signs to hang with tear slips that contained random compliments.

The top of the sign said *FREE, help yourself!* The slips had things like: "You are beautiful just the way you are!" "Who's smart? YOU! That's who!" and "Your smile lights a room up!" and more. She had asked her teacher if she could hang the sign by the water fountain so that the kids would see it and if they needed it they could take one. Her teacher said yes, of course, not really sure how fifth grade kids would respond. The teacher said she then sat back and watched as word of the sign spread around the room and students went one by one, under the pretense of getting a sip of water, but really to tear off a slip. She said she was amazed by the smiles that each of the children had on their faces as they walked back to their seats, each quietly folding their paper and putting it in their pocket, their book, inside their desk. By lunch, all the slips of paper were gone and the teacher said that the mood of the class was noticeably more positive. She said she was going to write a note but instead thought she would follow my daughter's lead and call me to give me a compliment.

"Your daughter is one of the most thoughtful and kind young people I have ever met! You are doing a really good job, mama!" she said to me. And when she hung up, I cried. They were 100 percent genuine happy tears! I had never felt so proud, so special, so much like a GOOD MOM in my life!

There are days, lots of days, when I really feel like I am blowing this whole working-mom thing. And then there are moments, when a teacher calls and tells you "GOOD JOB, MAMA" that, well, I feel like jumping up and doing an awesome dance. Perhaps we all need compliment signs with tear sheets attached so that we can remind each other, and ourselves, how special we are, that our shoes are cute, that our writing is awesome, and that we are doing a really good job raising our kids! Care to join me in an Awesome Dance?

About the Author:
Sharon Fuentes is an award-winning humor columnist, parenting guru, special needs advocate, co-author of *The Don't Freak Out Guide to Parenting Kids with Asperger's*, and is doing a really good job raising her kids! You can contact her at Sharon@sharonfuentes.com.

Figure 6. Mother and Daughter Photograph

Corporal Punishment
By Ajit Kumar Jha, India

When I was younger, I went to military school. In India, boys join at age of ten or eleven. These schools are known for disciplining kids with an iron hand, but they train you for a career in the armed forces, which guarantees you a respectable career and food for life. That's a lot in a country rife with poverty and short on equal opportunities. Back then, these schools treated children like adults. If you committed a minor infraction, you could be punished or worse yet, kicked out.

One day, while in an assembly, we noticed three bare-bodied boys standing on the dais. Each bore a placard, dangling from his neck declaring in bold: "Standing Here for Misconduct." Sights like these were rare. Most kids learned quickly not to cause any infraction.

Here we were all gathered to watch these boys stand, shamed in public. The assembly was gathered to watch. Our principal, a Lieutenant Colonel, came out on the dais in full military uniform. Taking out a piece of paper, he loudly proclaimed the misconduct committed. When we heard what these boys had done, we were all shocked...

These boys had been caught cheating on an exam. They had tried to pass papers during the All India

Secondary Board, one of senior exams needed to pass. During the exam, the proctor had caught them with little pieces of paper in their pockets… a foolish, childish thing to do. Something that could ruin your career before it began.

The physical training instructor came out next in full battle regalia, and behind him, a cane. The bare-bodied boys were asked to lie down to receive their punishment.

The external invigilator who had caught them red-handed was hell-bent on rusticating them, which meant not only would they lose one year, but they probably could never appear for the same exam. In other words, if the invigilator had his way, their careers would be ruined for good. The invigilator was so strict that he was not ready to listen to the voice of reason. He had the discretion to pardon them with a warning, but he said "No" once and for all.

The boys had made the cardinal mistake of entering into an argument with the invigilator. In addition, the two other boys aggressively entered into the fray in defense of their friend. On physical examination, all three were found to carry notes scribbled in small pieces of paper hidden in their pockets. The boys wanted to pass the higher secondary exam for which they had not studied. Unless they passed the higher secondary exam (Class XI), they were ineligible for the National Defense Academy.

When the matter reached the principal, he immediately decided on corporal punishment for these boys. That day, the principal also invited the invigilator to demonstrate to him how he dealt with indiscipline.

Before the boys were made to stand in the assembly, the principal made the invigilator have the boys run around the grounds and also do front rolls. Their shoulders and backs were already bruised by then. Next the principal came to the assembly with the invigilator in tow, where these poor boys were waiting to be caned. Each cane strike left a nasty bruise mark, while boys screamed in pain.

Barely had the exercise begun than the invigilator began sobbing. He rushed to intervene, holding the PTI's hand to stop it. To everyone's relief, the invigilator allowed the boys to appear in the exam. The seniors told us that our principal, Lt. Col. P.S. Satsangi had taken the harsh decision so as to save the career of these boys. While one among these boys went on to join the Merchant Navy, the other two joined the Defense Academy to emerge as the commissioned officers in the Indian Army.

Corporal punishment became a kind deed.

About the Author:

Ajit Kumar Jha studied Philosophy at St. Stephens College and Sociology at the Delhi School of Economics at Delhi

University. Currently, he works for different clients and also writes independently on different web platforms.

Figure 7. Lt. Col. PS. Satsangi

Figure 8. Military Academy

Eleanor

By Angelica Crawford, United Kingdom

I remember the first time I saw her. She was sitting there by the window, peaceful. I watched the sunlight stream down upon her delicate old face. Her wrinkles were defined by a golden hue, making her appear royal, ancient and wise. She seemed so graceful. I remember explaining to her that I was just visiting for the day – a spontaneous trip to the elderly care home. Smiling, she asked if I would like to join her for afternoon tea.

That day was the beginning of a beautiful friendship. Meeting Eleanor was one of the most important moments of my life, although I didn't know it at the time. She told me about her life and showed me pictures of her husband who had passed twelve years prior. I could see the devotion in her eyes as she reminisced about her years of blissful marriage. Eleanor was confined to a wheelchair, and at eighty-nine years of age she was unable to live alone. I could see that she was lonely. I wanted to help her feel loved again. It didn't take long for me to understand that Eleanor didn't need my pity, and I wasn't her superhero; she needed my friendship, and I was her companion.

My visits quickly grew from once a week to every other day. Eleanor and I would sit in the garden when the weather was nice and bask in the sunshine. We played cards, read stories and talked about life. Sometimes, we would sit silently and enjoy each other's company. I grew to cherish my time with Eleanor. Her age made her wise, and I respected her insight more than anyone.

The more time I spent with Eleanor, the more I grew to love her company just as much as she enjoyed mine. We became the best of friends in so short a time. Eleanor beamed with smiles whenever I walked through the door. Her nurse once told me that since I began visiting her, Eleanor was happier than she had been in years. I admit that I felt the same way. Eleanor was like my best friend and my grandmother. We enjoyed sharing little secrets about our lives and talked about our hopes and dreams. Our time together was always full of laughter and good conversation.

I remember feeling sad on many evenings after leaving Eleanor. Although she related her stories with animation and excitement, I couldn't help but feel sorry for her. It seemed as though all of her happy memories were in the past. I felt guilty. My life was so full of love, constant activity and new adventures. Sometimes I wondered if my visits were upsetting to her as they caused her to reminisce on her lifetime of memories. I see now that I was blind. Eleanor had been making new memories: new memories with me.

I remember the day I knew she was going to die. Eleanor was sitting in her usual spot by the window, but it wasn't sunny that day. Her face seemed to reflect the gloom and gray of the impending storm. She was tired, but wanted me to stay with her. We sat together in silence for quite a while, as we sometimes did. I remember her telling me in her usual grandmotherly voice that I should never stop loving and never give up. "You're a good woman," she said with a deep sincerity that I will never forget. I believe she knew that her end was near. I told Eleanor that I loved her, and she shed a tear while she whispered, "I love you too, my dear."

The next morning I received the call that Eleanor had passed. Part of me felt as though I had just lost my best friend, but I also felt grateful. I was grateful for Eleanor's friendship, for her love and kindness, insight and advice. It was then that I realized that Eleanor didn't just need me, but I needed her. She needed my ears to listen, my hands to hold, and my eyes to see into her soul. I never thought I could love someone so deeply who had been a stranger to me only five months previously.

Looking back, I know that I was meant to meet her, and my life will never be the same because of it. Knowing Eleanor changed me for the better. I wish I could have more time with her, but I have hope that I will one day see her again.

About the Author:

Angelica Crawford, twenty-three, is a writer, editor and tutor. She has a degree in English literature, and loves reading and writing short stories and articles. As a full-time mom and wife, Angelica enjoys spending time with her family and cooking new recipes.

Emergency Call
By Anna S., Oregon, USA

At a bank, I was distributing materials for a resource hotline. For those not familiar with it, a resource hotline is a telephone number that connects people in need with services that can help. People who need help often don't know where to go. So, the purpose of a hotline is to make people aware that resources are available to them. There are people who want to help!

To communicate our services and convince the bank to distribute our pamphlets to the public, I had just made a brief presentation. Afterwards, a staff member followed me to my car. She surprised me.

"I wanted to say thank you," she said, looking into my eyes. "I've used the resource line before…" She looked like she wanted to say something more. "It is important that people know about it."

Two years prior, she had barely escaped a violent marriage. She and her husband had a son who was four at the time. The abuse had begun sometime after he was born. She told me she stayed in the marriage because she had nowhere else to go. Without a job, car, money, or family, she thought staying was better – it meant her son would have a roof over his head, food to eat, and clothes to wear.

"If we left," she said, "we would be homeless."

Then, everything changed.

One afternoon, she put a cartoon on for her son while she took a quick shower. While she was showering, she heard the door slam and the television turn off. Before she could react, she heard her son scream. As any mother would, she ran out quickly to protect her child. She jumped in front of a brawl and was punished. That night, the abuse she received was even more severe. Afterwards, she crawled into her son's room, spending the night on the floor cradling him... She knew she had to do something because she realized then they were not safe in their own home.

The next morning, as soon as she heard her husband leave, she grabbed what she could carry. She picked up her son and walked out the door. In her purse, she had just nine dollars, to the cent. The need for action was immediate. She had no choice, no recourse, and no alternative. Every day the beatings had only gotten worse and now her son was in danger.

As they walked through the neighborhood, she tried to figure out what to do next. She took her son to the park, hoping it would help her come up with a plan. How would she feed them? Where could she go? Eventually, they boarded a bus and rode around town. Five hours passed and she still wasn't sure what to do. She had no family to help her. She knew no one who wasn't a mutual friend. On the surface her husband was the perfect gentleman, would anyone even believe her? Eventually, she went into a large grocery store and wandered the aisles...

Throughout the day, no one looked her in the eye. Maybe they didn't want to get involved. Her face looked like she'd been in a heavyweight boxing match. Her son was scared. She couldn't stop crying.

And then a young woman, an employee, noticed her. She asked if she needed help. Initially, she said "no" because she felt embarrassed, but the young woman smiled gently and said, "If you need to call anyone, please, feel free to use the phone. It's located in the back of the store."

She didn't know whom to call but she went back there anyway because she figured it would be out of sight. Within minutes the young employee came around the corner with the information for the resource line and said, "I'd like to help you make this call." And she did.

Together they found an emergency shelter and transportation to get them there. While they were waiting, the young employee gathered donations from the staff and store and put together a care package of food, toiletries, socks, and two warm sweatshirts.

"The best gift ever," she said. "I've learned a lot of things over the past four years: how to take care of myself, how to manage and save money. I have a great job and my son is doing well in school. But what I've learned most is how kindness can change your life."

About the Author:
Anna S. is the pen name of an American writer. She lives in Oregon with her family, where she was born and raised.

Fallen Angel
By Anthony Ford, London, UK

Morning had flown by. Lunch time was almost over. I hurried back to work, lost in my racing thoughts. The queue at the bank was too long. I barely had time to bite into a random sandwich dashed from the cafe. There was no time for coffee... Not only was I running late, there were pressing issues to be dealt with when I got back. There were more numbers to call, a deadline to keep and payments past due. The last thing I needed was a distraction.

Of course, my route was stopped short. A baby bird sat on the sidewalk ahead, a soft fluffy mess on the pavement. It stood in front of my giant foot that almost stamped down in my rush... At first, I stepped over it and made a few feet forwards. Time was pressing, I would be late. I had needs of my own. Stopping would lead me to more problems to resolve. But, from the corner of my eye, I saw it...

The tiny creature continued to sit and paid me no mind as it looked to the sky, calling to the above. Newly arrived on this earth, just broken free, struggling to fly, its plight made mine pale by comparison. Suddenly, I felt kinship and great empathy for this creature. I, too, was confused, worried, lost... I, tangled in a maze of thoughts;

it, a prisoner of circumstance. "*Out of the mouth of babes and sucklings thou hast perfected praise.*" (Matthew 21:16)

Slowly, my legs moved backwards on their own. I crept up to the wee creature, leaning down to study it, trying not to threaten it with my size. Smaller than a golf ball, I could make out its tiny face and now hear its low chirping. It was a baby blue tit with blue fluttering wings. Its yellow chest was proud and beautiful. Its black bandit mask was decorated with the smallest yet shiniest jewel eyes I had ever seen.

Looking around in either direction, I saw vastness. Stretched the long empty urban street with rows of cars; there was no other human or living creature. Looking at my watch, I saw the minute-hand tick. It was so late... Yet, the bird was there chirping, mesmerizing, and in need.

Crouching down alongside it, I held out my hand. Without hesitation, the little bird stepped on to the hollow of my palm and sat down. Shocked by its confidence, I believe the bird knew I was there for it. The world seemed endlessly connected.

Now I had a problem, what to do? I had a bird in the palm of my hand. This small bird placed its trust in me – its life was now literally in my hands.

To say I was nervous is an understatement.

Think! I commanded myself as I looked around me frantically searching for ideas. Most fortuitously, my eyes caught a glimpse of a house nearby with a small front garden. A large bush thrust up to the sky and hung over the wooden fence bordering it. Beyond, there lay a giant brown terracotta potted plant. While looking thusly, I heard it...

Amongst the stems and branches came unmistakable chirping. Moving closer, I was able to see struggling movements inside the large bush. Inching even closer, I saw another chick, obviously newly hatched, and very similar to the one I held in my hand. It had to be a relative! The small bird I held had possibly hatched first, leading the charge.

Had it attempted to fly?

Then, fallen from the bush and landed on the sidewalk? Immediately, I walked towards the open gate, up the path, and cut over a lawn to approach the large bush from a better angle. I realized this was the best place to set down the small creature. It would be up off the ground, above any predatory or careless animals such as trekking humans, and close to home.

Stepping up to the pot and crouching down, I held my arm out. Gingerly, I placed the fluffy chick on the top soil of the pot by scooting it off my palm. Surprisingly, I noticed it had fallen asleep. Possibly, in the heat of my hand, it had found comfort and succumbed to slumber thinking it was near its mother. *There are times when you can sleep and times when you can't,*" I whispered as I nudged the small bird awake "... *and right now, you can't!*" It suddenly awoke and began again to chirp. I placed it down and it continued to squawk. The other chick above chirped back. I watched as they instantly recognized each other and, I imagine, a conversation of sorts began. I smiled, turned and left them to it...

A week or so went by until I found myself striding along the same sidewalk toward work. On occasion, I did wonder what happened to him. In the early morning I had gotten off the bus one stop before usual in favor of a brisk walk. As I approached the particular area, a harmony of birdsong, chirping and whistling filled the air. Birds swooped across the street from rooftop to rooftop then back and only until I was half way down the street did the sounds quieten and disappear.

At first, I had my doubts as to what had actually happened but soon forgot as another workday began. The following day, I repeated my journey this time with a work colleague who happened to join me as we strolled along. Once again, the birdsong suddenly erupted at the very same spot. As my colleague was talking, she immediately halted midsentence as her words were lost amid the avalanche of squawks and whistles. As the small birds flew in numbers back and forth she physically stopped and looked around as I smiled...

"Don't worry," I said. "They are just saying hello."

"Eh?" she asked.

We turned and continued to walk. "Well, I was coming back from lunch one time and on the sidewalk ahead I saw a small bird..."

About the Author:

Anthony Ford is a writer/actor and lives in London. He has worked on stage in the UK's Royal National Theatre alongside Sir Ian McKellen. He acted in a Trevor Nunn production of Ibsen's *An Enemy of the People*. As a writer, he focuses on screenplays and short stories and has written two novels. His latest screenplay was completed last year and is entitled *End-Line, a Christmas thriller*. At the moment it is under development with the production company Caramie Productions Ltd. for a movie feature film.

Far From Home
By Rachel De Bretagne, France

I wasn't always as miserable, though on that particular day, it felt like the world was against me. It is hard to put on a brave face day after day and pretend to like the party life. Losing myself in a glass of alcohol was actually easier than facing up to the fact that I was homesick, heartbroken, and had no faith left in life. Having hitchhiked to a foreign country to marry my childhood sweetheart, it had been a shock to see that he was settled into the party life with someone else. That stung.

The short man that came into the piazza looked ordinary. He was your average customer, would order a drink to cool him down from the hot sun, and then walk out of the piazza. I would still be here, stuck in a life I didn't want because someone I loved betrayed me. I didn't have the money to go home, and even if I did, what was there to go home to?

"Hi," he said. "Why so sad?"

Somehow he had picked up on my sadness when people don't usually. I don't usually drop the mask long enough for people to get inside it. This was an exception. The sun was hot and I was working alone. Somehow that part of me that was so miserable must have surfaced.

"I'm sorry," I exclaimed. "I really didn't mean to appear so sad."

I placed the practiced smile back on my face as I took his order. Of course, it was the same as yesterday and the day before. Life wasn't moving on. It was at a standstill.

"Is there anything I can do to make your life happier?" he said, with startling ease.

I didn't know if this was a bold attempt to make me smile, a pick-up line, or a genuine offer. Looking down at his finger, I could see the wedding band clearly, so it wasn't a chat-up line. So many times, people say things that are hollow, and he chose the wrong moment to play with my head.

"You could buy me a ticket to go home." I said, laughingly.

"Where's home?" he asked.

"I come from England," I replied. "You know, that place where it always rains."

I never thought any more about it for the next week. In fact, as the summer sun got hotter in the sky, I tried to hide the way I felt by losing myself in a book on the beach. The breezes always felt good and on the rocky crags, I could get away from everyone and just be alone with my thoughts. Tears came involuntarily. I never knew you could cry lying down, but when the build-up of unhappiness is so much, tears don't care how they come out.

When he appeared again in the café later in the week, I greeted him with the normal nonchalant smile reserved for people whom I thought merited it. He was a nice guy and although he couldn't help me out of my predicament, he still seemed pleasant enough to talk to.

"Hi," he said in greeting.

"Good morning to you," I replied.

This time, I served him his drink without asking what he wanted, as I already knew. The sun was blisteringly hot so what else would the man want but a cool martini with oodles of ice? People don't pay for their drinks until they go, but as he stood to leave, he called me over. This wasn't out of the ordinary as waitresses usually took the money for the drinks. My tray in my hand ready to collect empty glasses, I approached as I always did.

"And this is for you," he said, putting the money onto the tray along with a white envelope.

I looked at the envelope in curiosity.

"Don't open it until later when you finish," he said.

From that moment until this moment, I never saw him again. What he had put onto my tray was the means to get home. He had gone out of his way to find out my details from my boss, and had been out to the airport to buy me a ticket.

This may not seem like an awful lot to readers, but it was a ticket that changed my view about what life has to offer. Sometimes opportunities lie in waiting when you least expect them. Sometimes, you're taught to give as much as you get, and I eventually got back on my feet in London and traced the man by email and was able to repay him. It was more than just a random act of kindness. It was an act which opened up the doors of possibility to me and gave me back belief that there are good people in life. I no longer needed to hide behind alcohol or the mask of a smile. As I walked toward the airport that day, the smile was a very genuine one I hadn't felt for a very long time and the lightness within my heart told me the world waited for me to embrace it rather than locking it out. It taught me to be open to possibilities rather than slamming the door on hope.

That's what made the event so life-changing and so very important. When you experience goodness that asks for nothing in return, you are humbled by it and it is that humility that makes you open to seeing those flowers in the springtime, rather than just passing them by with eyes too tired to look. I took up the challenge of living life to the full, because of one random act of generosity on the part of a stranger. There is no other reason. The kindness may come in many guises as life has now taught me, and it is recognizing opportunities as they arise that shapes the people we become.

I often wonder what happened to the man in the café, but most of all would like to tell him that his act of kindness was life-changing, though people like him don't need acknowledgement. They are just as happy knowing they did something nice for another human being, without the need for thanks.

About the Author:

Born in the UK, Rachel De Bretagne is widely travelled and now lives in southern France where she has found happiness and contentment and is learning to play the guitar. Her life has been shaped by acts of kindness though she strongly believes in giving kindness back to others, or "paying it forward."

Farewell Lullaby
By Joyce Jacobo, California, USA

"Our lives our not our own. From womb to tomb, we are bound to others, past and present, and by each crime and every kindness, we birth our future." - Unknown

A light drizzle fell that late midsummer afternoon, when my family reached the neighborhood in Riverside where my grandparents lived. Most homes there were worn two-story structures standing tall like proud military veterans along a gradual slope, and American flags hanging at each doorstep. Maybe it was the numbness possessing me that made it feel this way, but it seemed like our blue van crept through the empty streets in slow motion. I could barely register anything, aside from the raindrops sliding down the car windows and the whispering echo of the news that my grandmother would soon leave us.

Several relatives had already parked against the curb before the house, and we eased in behind them to complete the line. My parents led the way over the dried grass to the porch and rang the doorbell. I could see faint light flickering in the living room and shadowy forms shifting inside. One moved to answer the door – my aunt, who quickly ushered us inside.

The room had been cleared to make way for the medical bed where my Grandma Jacobo lay too still under her white sheets. A doctor was checking her pulse and talking in a low voice to my grandfather and encircling aunts and uncles.

My eleven-year-old mind had trouble making sense of the scene. It was wrong. We had visited our grandparents many, many times over the years. Several of my earliest memories revolved around gathering in the living room – with shelves filled with glass figurines, knickknacks, and clocks that played fanciful tunes every hour – to celebrate holidays, and birthdays, and grand occasions with laughter and joy. We took group photographs here, exchanged stories here. It was always where I would cuddle on the couch between Grandma and my mother, feeling safe and content.

I couldn't bear to think about how that all would change. So while the doctor spoke privately with the grownups, I broke away and wandered into the dining room. There was the small wooden table where the whole family would converge to have big feasts, sing songs, or discuss various topics. Sometimes I would feel out of place amid the boisterous proceedings, but whenever this happened, Grandma had a way of detecting it and helping me to belong again. She would invite me into the narrow kitchen and smuggle me sugar cookies and milk, or sit beside me on a bench that allowed us a widespread view of the sloping neighborhood below.

Looking through these darkened rooms, I realized how much Grandma had figured into my memories of each room in the house. I saw myself at the wooden table, crinkling my nose at macaroni and cheese that had small noodles (which I insisted should have been big) – and then Grandma sitting down next to me and coaxing in her usual soft, chirping voice:

"Macaroni is delicious, *mi hija*, with noodles of any size."

The memory faded into the shadows, replaced by the sounds of the rain growing heavier outside, leaving me frozen in place until my mom beckoned from the threshold to the living room. I entered in time to see the doctor and Grandpa exchange blessings at the door, before the physician nodded gravely to the rest of us and left.

The gentle hands of our relatives guided my older brother and me to Grandma's bedside, one by one.

An aunt whispered in my ear, "Don't say goodbye, or you might scare her."

With this warning, I came to stand next to my grandma. She failed to move or open her eyes at my quiet greeting. It was hard to tell whether or not Grandma could hear me. I had never been so helpless, and what hurt more than anything was knowing that after all the wonderful things Grandma had done for me, from her kind words, to her warm embraces, to simply being *my* Grandma Jacobo, I could give her nothing comparable in return.

How could you repay someone who had meant the world to you, the very last time you knew you would see them, when you were not supposed to say goodbye? Like a miracle, a small idea occurred to me.

"Could I sing a song for Grandma?" I asked my parents.

"Yes," my mom replied, alongside several consenting murmurs.

"This song is called 'Your Heart Will Lead You Home,'" I told Grandma.

The room fell silent, and I began to sing. It was a tune I had heard recently in a Disney cartoon – *The Tigger Movie*, letting Tigger of the Hundred Acre Woods know he had a home among his loved ones forever, who would continue to care for him no matter where he might roam, or for how long. That had been the meaning I carried away from the movie, and the lyrics never said goodbye. Instead, they conveyed unending devotion and comfort.

This was how I bid farewell to Grandma, and throughout the melody a hundred emotions and memories swirled within me. My voice stayed steady. I forgot about the rest of the family standing in the room. While the music lasted, it was just Grandma and me, and I was singing to her for the first and last time. Tears sprung to my eyes and dripped down my cheeks, but I pressed on to end. The last few words reverberated in the thin air, and the spell shattered.

I could hardly stand. All the energy had flooded out of me. My mom placed a hand on my shoulder, and I noticed other members of the family watching with tears glistening as well.

I turned my attention back to Grandma.

She was smiling.

About the Author:

Joyce Jacobo is a writer who hails from a small countryside paradise in Southern California. She holds a B.A. in Literature & Writing Studies from Cal State San Marcos and plans to begin the graduate program there in the fall. Among her fondest wishes are to make people happy through her work, create imaginative worlds and characters, and point out the wonders that surround everyone in the world.

Figure 9. Grandma Jacobo by Jesus Jacobo, Jr. (Husband)

Fatherhood

By Jules Whitney, Oregon, USA

There is this old cliché about fatherhood: The first time you hold your newborn in your arms, something inside of you changes, as if there is a click – your previously self-serving, haphazard, ill-fitting moral gears suddenly align, and you find yourself wholly subordinated to the whimsical demands of this tiny creature. The birth of a child rescues you from your own existential angst – if we are all night travelers in a vast, endless desert, she is a star in the sky by which to navigate. You get a direction. You get a purpose.

It is a cliché because it is true – but it's not really a "click," and it's not even instantaneous. I can tell you exactly what it felt like: sheer, unadulterated, unending terror.

Terror, because I was holding a child I had created with a woman whom I was divorcing (unbeknownst to us when we were conducting the wildly oscillating, heart-wrenching business of separation – screaming matches until two in the morning, nights spent sleeping in the car, moving possessions in and out and in and out of the house – she had just become pregnant). Terror, because my mere, meager income came from a job ripping up flooring in rental properties during the mornings, for nine bucks an hour under the table, and forcibly bouncing drunk UFC enthusiasts from a local bar on weekend nights. Terror, because I lived on my best friend's couch in an infested, tiny one-bedroom apartment surrounded by a complex full of meth cookers, petty thugs and Chinese "restaurants" that served barely edible food in the front and laundered drug money in the back. Terror, because my life had thus far been a fever dream of playing in a rock band, working low-paying jobs, and filling my face with as much cocaine as I could – I had dropped out of high school, never held a job longer than a year, had no skills, no work ethic, and no idea how to be a man. How would I ever learn how to be a father?

I was an f***up without a shred of common sense. But when I stood in that fluorescent-lit hospital room and felt my daughter's unbearably insubstantial weight in my arms, I knew I was long overdue to learn how to be a man. I told my soon-to-be ex-wife that I was going to join the army.

It was 2006, at the height of the Iraq War, when American forces were sustaining some of their heaviest fighting – and casualties. An old friend of mine, who was a former marine, pointed out a single, simple statistic: Nearly all of the men and women killed or maimed in combat were soldiers in the army. A marine infantryman, though just as frequently exposed to danger, had less of a chance of being injured in theater than a civilian did driving on the I-5 freeway. Call it training, call it culture, call it whatever: Marines died less often.

I certainly didn't want to die – I was joining the military to learn how to *live*. So, I drove to the Marine Corps recruitment station a little north of where I lived (ironically, I took the 5.) There, I met Gunnery Sergeant Lopez, whom I might describe in any other circumstances as a "pistol," if she hadn't been an expert rifleman. At thirty-eight years old and five foot two inches, she might have weighed 115 pounds if you filled her pockets with rocks. She was a child of immigrants from the Dominican Republic and had skin the color of cloves; she had huge eyes that got even wider when she was amused or angry, muscles that stood out from her body like rope, and a mouth full of perfect, glittering-white teeth. She had a master's degree in military history, was an expert fixed-wing mechanic, and a career recruiter in the United States Marine Corps – and was a mother to two boys, thirteen and nine.

I introduced myself and asked her how quickly I could leave for boot camp. Her voice was halting, low and sharp, and she clicked her teeth when she finished a sentence, as though for punctuation.

"What makes you think you can be a marine?" she asked.

"Can we skip the bull****?" I replied.

I told her about my daughter. I told her about my current employment situation. I told her that my ex-wife and new daughter had no health insurance and that we now had a $13,000 bill just for my little girl's birth – and more charges were rolling in by the week. She produced a stack of paperwork and I started affixing my signature to page after page of documents – forms of consent to release my medical information, forms to state that I understood policies and procedures, forms pledging my life and sacred honor to the United States Marine Corps.

A few days later, she called me into the recruitment office. My medical records, she explained, showed a history of mental health issues, including behavioral trouble, severe attention deficit disorder, and most importantly, depression – the demon that had haunted every long night, every dream of the future, every relationship I had since I was old enough to remember. She explained that my mental health history, combined with my failure to complete high school, made me an ineligible candidate for the marine corps.

I nodded and sighed. "Is that it, then?" I asked.

She asked me if I had ever been suicidal. I responded that I had. She asked me if I had ever tried to kill myself. I responded that I had. She asked me whether I thought I would ever do it again. I said, "No."

She said, "What's different?"

I said, "I'm a father now."

This was the first kindness that Gunnery Sergeant Lopez showed me: She removed the pages from my medical records that documented my depression, put them into a folder and gave them to me. Then, she filed the rest of my package.

Shortly thereafter, my aptitude test results came in. I could be an electrical engineer and leave for boot camp in two months. I asked her how I could leave within the week. She told me I could become a cook. So, I signed up as a cook and shipped out five days later.

As I traversed the myriad hellish tortures of boot camp, I sent as much money to my ex-wife as I could. I missed my daughter every day, and thought of her throughout physical training, marching drills, classrooms and conditioning hikes. I left before she was even two months old – at times, I could barely remember what she looked like – but merely knowing that she needed me gave me the will to persevere.

Unfortunately, I was still only a private – the lowest-paid, lowest-ranking marine there is – and I was not making enough money to both provide for my daughter and pay down the debt her mother and I had incurred in bringing her into the world.

When I arrived home after twelve weeks at the marine corps recruit depot in San Diego, I discovered that my recruiter had retired from military service. Before she left, however, she showed me the great random act of kindness that led me to write this story.

Gunnery Sergeant Lopez spent her last weeks in the marine corps contacting several agencies on my behalf – most importantly, the Navy and Marine Corps Relief Society, a medical charity for service members, and the hospital where my daughter was born. She had secured donations, payments and debt forgiveness to the tune of $10,500 – almost the entire bill for my daughter's birth. I had enough left in the bank after three months in boot camp to pay the rest and start my career in the marines on solid financial footing.

Gunnery Sergeant Lopez married and changed her name, so I was never able to track her down and thank her. But I will not – I could not – ever forget her incredible generosity toward the fat, sensitive, artsy loser that showed up and asked to leave for boot camp as quickly as possible. I will never be able to repay her kindness; I can only hope to pay it forward to someone in the future.

About the Author:
Jules Whitney is the pen name of a former marine turned writer and journalist. He lives with his daughter in Portland, Oregon.

First Night in Bangkok
By Steven Brooks, Manchester, England

Jumping out of the taxi, we felt like fish out of water. A possible contribution to this: the first thing our feet felt was the cool splash of the puddle near the curb. Despite this minor grievance, my friend and I stood there mostly amazed and literally soaking in the sights. The smells, sounds, and exotic oriental scenery penetrated our senses within seconds. Having never left the most European of countries before, this place across the other side of world was the stuff of dreams and wonder. It was so rich, vibrant, fragrant and alive in every way imaginable. Personally, I felt like a gopher that discovered the other side of the ocean lying beyond a stream.

Although it was still dark outside, the buzzing electric lights lit up the streets with activity. From experience of city living, I knew the twilight hours of the day opened up a new realm of activity during the evenings. Drinkers, dancers, hustlers – the good and the bad – occupy the city streets, seeking adventures of all types. Skulking in the dark, they wait for natural light to end before coming out to play. Though beautiful at dusk, things could easily turn seedy quickly.

Of course, I was forewarned to be on guard and perhaps this contributed to my sense of hypervigilance.

From what I had learned in Europe, visiting a new land can be dangerous as opportunists prey on the naive. Criminal elements dwell in the dark. Sometimes you lose what's in your pocket, but other times, that makes you lucky if that's all you've lost.

From the airport all the way in to Bangkok, my friend and I had our faces pressed to the glass. Now, we were finally in the presence of the actual sites, and no longer just observers, but participants in the buzz of the frenzied city. Car and truck drivers seemed fine as they drove at a sensible pace (of course, we were in a moving vehicle alongside them when we watched them). On foot, local folk zipped by at lightning speeds – mostly on mopeds, dangerously enough to put me off hiring a scooter, ever. Never had I seen anything like it.

Three or even four people would sit squashed together in a single 50cc automatic. The amount of luggage some of these people could carry with them was incredible, too. I, for one, was completely gobsmacked. One man, on the back of a moped, was carrying a bicycle with him! I instantly pictured him on a road in England being pulled over by the police.

Departing the taxi, my friend and I paid 400 baht, which we thought was quite reasonable considering the twenty miles or so we had just travelled. Being in a new place and exhausted by our lengthy travels, we had a number of priorities first among which, notably, was to find shelter. Also, we instinctively (through conditioning) wanted to dispose of our luggage before we were pickpocketed – just as a precaution. Unfortunately, the taxi driver hadn't taken us all the way to Khaosan Road, our intended destination, which was a little annoying as we were both fatigued and didn't know our way about.

As we approached Khaosan Road, the sounds raced into my ears like a fleet of beetles evading the pursuit of a hose pipe. This place was absolutely incredible; however, I was still anxious to drop my gear off. A combination of music, traffic, and mutterings from people of all nationalities was a true assault on my senses. Even though sleep would have been the smarter thing to pursue on this first night of landing, I wanted to go out and soak up this new culture.

At the top end of Khaosan Road, I noticed a Burger King opposite us and declared to myself that I wouldn't be touching one of those for a long time. (This turned out to be a lie, as I purchased one out of hunger and familiarity.) As we were about to make the left turn down Khaosan Road, an elderly Thai lady approached me looking a little distressed. She didn't speak English but her problem was clear.

She was a bit of a cripple physically and was having trouble kickstarting the ignition on her motorbike. Before I had thought twice, I handed my bag to my friend and offered my assistance. I'm not sure why I did this, except maybe a sudden burst of latent chivalry took over. As soon as I did, though, I began to feel regret as the cynic in me became convinced she was going to accuse me of breaking her bike.

What a start, eh? First night in Thailand and I'm getting swindled by one of the local pensioners. Perfect! My tiredness made me irritable. Nonetheless, I had offered to help. It took me two or three tries to get the engine to tick over. Once that occurred, I was eager to leave. I had convinced myself not to trust anything or anyone based on first appearances and I'd managed to screw that parameter along with the burger promise up on my first night. Thus, I was quite shocked when I didn't get robbed or mugged or tricked.

Back in the UK, most people who were rescued thus would simply thank you and then shoot off. Judging by the depth and sincerity of this lady's gratitude, she must have been trying all day to start her engine. Immediately after she had thrown her arms around my neck, I was overwhelmed. I also felt a little excited and began to think about travelling the country and doing good deeds for cute women. Never have I been met with such a moving degree of praise and adulation. She was almost in tears!

Once she finally took her arms off me, she gave me one more sign of gratitude by placing her hands together and wishing me well. It was obvious from the look in the eyes of this frail lady that she was utterly appreciative and that brought joy to my heart. I had not been in Bangkok for an hour yet, but helping that woman totally changed my attitude within just those sixty minutes. That single experience taught me to relax and appreciate that innocence is all around us. One good deed ended up being a gift back unto itself. Maybe that's why they say it is better to give than receive?

About the Author:
Steven Brooks is a writer from Manchester, England. After having his first poem published at the tender age of twelve, he spent most of his teenage years writing hip-hop music before going on to study media. He started writing comedy while at university and after graduating, started writing professionally. His biggest ambition is to become successful as a DJ and music producer, and he continues to write as much as possible.

A Hero's Heart

By Darko, Serbia

One beautiful Sunday on a late winter morning that felt more like spring, an eleven-year-old girl decided to go rollerblading. The weather was nice and bright, a perfect moment to go out and enjoy the pleasures of youth. Smiling and being a generally happy and active little girl, neither this youngster nor any of her guardians could anticipate how a tragedy could soon strike.

In the same area she played in, her neighbors possessed a large bullmastiff, affectionately yet appropriately named Bear. Normally, the massive guard dog sat stationary as a well-trained sentry. Occasionally, he would tug at his collar, but remained chained at the neck by his strong leather leash. Unfortunately, on that same fine Sunday morning, Bear broke free.

Without much warning, he ran directly into the street and attacked the little girl. Viciously, he bit into her arm. His fangs sank without mercy and tossed the little girl around as if she were a rag doll. It was horrifying. She was screaming and bleeding, but the bullmastiff just wouldn't let go. Witnesses tried to chase him away, to scare him with sticks and whatever they could find, but it was to no avail. Bear would not let go. Terrified, the little girl's neighbors heard the commotion. Frantically rushing out, they tried to help, unsure of how to assist without getting injured themselves. But the little girl's dachshund, a small but fiercely loyal wiener dog, Leo, was faster. Valiantly, Leo started barking and attacking the bullmastiff despite being at least four times smaller. After a few moments of being ignored, Leo succeeded in distracting the bullmastiff. The big dog let go of the girl and shifted his focus to little Leo.

Leo was relentless and fought with all his heart. He took on the out-of-control bullmastiff when no one else was able. He was able to rescue the little girl from suffering worse injuries, and potentially even death.

When all the people that gathered finally succeeded in mustering up their courage and chasing the bullmastiff away, little Leo lay still. His eyes were clear and smart, but his belly and spine had suffered horrific injury. His tiny body was damaged. Trying to stand up, he quivered and fell to the ground. Neighbors quickly took the little girl to hospital where she got received some stitches; no permanent damage had been done. At the cost of his own peril, the loyal dog had saved his owner.

Quickly, the neighbors convened to take Leo to the public clinic. However, they were turned down at the door. After that, Leo was sped to a private vet.

Hearing his courageous tale, the doctors there did everything they could to try to save his life, including performing surgery on him for almost three hours.

His prognosis was dire but the doctor in charge was optimistic, especially the day after surgery when our little hero wiggled his tail. Leo clearly was a fighter – but he was not invincible. Sadly, he ultimately succumbed to his injuries and was buried under the tree in his owner's backyard. Leo was just a week shy of two years old, still a young pup.

The people of Panchevo, Serbia, were so moved by the act of this heroic dog that they felt they needed to do something. Subsequently, they petitioned town hall to make a statue of Leo for display in the town square. Social networks spread the story. Later this year, our little hero will have a real hero's goodbye. His memory will be preserved.

Thank you, Leo, thank you for reminding us why this world still deserves a chance. Sometimes you don't need big muscles, super speed, or a large body or invincibility to be a hero. Sometimes all you need is a hero's heart.

About the Author:
Darko is a twenty-five-year-old writer from Serbia. He plays American football, loves video games, and of course, books.

Heroes in an Unlikely Place
By Lisa Martin, New York, USA

Note: In the case of some individuals, names have been changed to protect privacy.

"If you're an underdog, mentally disabled, physically disabled, if you don't fit in, if you're not as pretty as the others, you can still be a hero." – Steve Guttenberg

&

When I was working in the field of mental health, people I knew would tell me that I was a special person, a "hero," for working with these individuals. I always responded by saying that my work was meaningful: that helping others was such a rewarding experience. Historically, persons suffering from mental illness have been stigmatized. They have often been perceived as aggressive and violent, but my experience taught me otherwise. I learned to see beyond the labels and to embrace these individuals as a whole. Having a mental illness does not make a person bad. It just means that they have an additional set of challenges they need to overcome. In addition, many persons suffering from mental illness have been abused in their past. Some of the most famous people in this world have had mental illnesses: Beethoven, Charles Dickens, and Sylvia Plath, to name a few. They have been able to make a difference in this world despite their own mental illness. The story I am about to tell you is one more extraordinary example.

Years ago, I worked as an assistant manager in a residential facility for persons suffering from serious and persistent mental illnesses such as bipolar disorder, major depressive disorder, and schizoaffective disorder. The residence was located on a busy city street that was often filled with vehicular and pedestrian traffic. One cold fall day, there was a torrential downpour, the type that falls horizontally and renders an umbrella practically useless. To make things worse, the wind was blowing fiercely. It was the kind of day that makes one reluctant to leave the house.

One of the residents, Maxine, had gone out to the porch to have a cigarette. Maxine was a petite woman in her thirties, suffering from schizophrenia. While she was having her cigarette, she discovered that a stranger had fallen on the ground in front of the house. Alarmed, she enlisted the help of two other residents. Together, the three carried the man out of the rain and onto the porch. They promptly notified staff, and an ambulance was called. The man was shivering, so the residents proceeded to give him dry clothing and put his wet clothes in the washer. One of the residents even gave the man a pair of their own shoes so that he could have dry feet. All the while, the three residents continued to assist and support the stranger. The man was greatly touched by their kindness. He reported that he had been suffering from a serious medical condition that affected his ability to walk. The man was finally taken away in the ambulance. Several days later he came back to return the borrowed clothing and thank the residents who had helped him in his time of need. Subsequently, I did a little write-up in the staff newsletter about the kind actions of these three persons. I offered to use their names, but they chose to remain anonymous.

I often wonder how many cars passed by on that busy street, ignoring the man who had fallen on the ground that day. I would like to think that the drivers just didn't see him, but something tells me otherwise. There is no knowing how long this man would have lain outside in the heavy rain had it not been for the actions of these three residents. Heroes come in all shapes and sizes, and they don't always come dressed in a costume complete with capes, rippling muscles or fantastic superpowers. They often come from unlikely places.

About the Author
Lisa Martin has a Master of Arts degree in psychology, and worked in the field of mental health for nearly a decade.

She is now a freelance web designer and copywriter. She lives with her husband and dog in Rochester, New York.

The Homeless and the Strays
By Ivana Milakovic, Serbia

The news broadcasts we see are scary. All we talk about nowadays are wars, murders, and other frightening events. If you looked at the reporting of current events, the world is an ugly terrible place, and we are on the verge of disaster. We are a disaster. But when I go outside, that's not what I see. Of course, I do see people misbehaving – but I also see kindness and greatness. I see beauty even from those who seemingly have the least to give. Humanity is more than our most horrific crimes. Our goodness outshines that. We don't talk about that enough.

For example: One day, I was standing in the checkout line in the local grocery store. Bored, I looked around. Behind me was a stressed-out-looking woman with a full shopping basket. Behind her was a man without a basket who was holding just a small bag of dry cat food. He looked like a homeless guy, middle-aged, maybe older. At the same time, he looked like he had no worries in the world, patiently waiting among the impatient shoppers.

It was my turn. I paid for the groceries and got out. In front of the grocery store, there was an alley cat. It was probably a tom, and quite dirty, but healthy-looking. Loving creatures, I greeted the cat. It meowed loudly, but when it realized I had nothing for him, he decided to ignore me.

Cats.

Suddenly, I recalled the man in the checkout. I wondered... I was in no hurry, so I waited to see if my suspicions were true. Sure enough, the homeless man exited the grocery store and greeted the cat. Pulling out the small bag, he invited him to eat. The tom meowed and followed him up a small hill to a more secluded place, where he could devour his meal in peace.

Up the hill they went, the two homeless guys, one walking on two legs, the other walking on four and covered with fur, both looking as if the world was theirs. From their point of view, it probably was.

Another day, in another part of the town, I had lunch with my mother. On my way home, I passed by a small park. I saw a homeless woman walking slowly through the park toward a bench. A small black three-legged dog followed her, wagging his tail enthusiastically. The dog didn't really seem to expect anything, he was just happy to be with her and to follow her. Two friends going to have a sit in a park on a pleasant, sunny day.

I don't think I've ever seen a happier dog.

The woman got to the bench and sat. The dog sat on the ground next to her, still happy, still wagging his tail. The woman reached into her dress pocket and dug out a piece of bread about the size of a fist. She split the bread in two and gave one half to the dog. She ate her part, the dog ate his. The homeless woman relaxed on the bench, and the dog relaxed on the ground next to her feet.

People in an expensive restaurant don't look that happy after a delicious meal. And yet, for the two friends in the park, a piece of bread and some sun were enough.

Sharing and kindness make the difference.

I never talked to those people. I only watched them go about their daily lives. Nonetheless, they taught me something anyway. They taught me that the world is a beautiful place if you look around you. Sharing and kindness are everywhere. There is beauty in the world. It doesn't cost money. It won't get you awards or prizes. You won't be splashed on the newspaper page for it.

The world isn't just scary – it's also full of kind people. We just need to open our eyes and we'll see them. Hopefully, we can learn something from them. We can learn to be generous and good. We can have the good outweigh the bad.

About the Author:

Ivana Milakovic is a writer and translator from Belgrade, Serbia. She is the published author of a short story collection called *Cat Dreams*, two educational television series for preschoolers, and 7,000+ articles on various topics, mostly inspirational in some way. She is taking historical fencing lessons and attempts to befriend every cat she sees.

Figure 10. Alley cats: man's best friend.

How a Puppy Taught Me to Live
By Dejan Savanovic, Bosnia and Herzegovina

We often forget how precious life and every moment of it is. Instead of living in the present, we burden ourselves by re-examining the past and worrying about the future. At certain rare moments, our pets remind us how lucky we are to be right here and right now, with them in the present. This is a story about one of those moments, about a puppy I saved from the cold and, although it couldn't return the favor or say "thanks," I was rewarded for this act in a way I never expected or thought possible.

I live in a small town, high up in the mountains. On a clear day, I can see humidity from the forests on hills around the town evaporate and go straight into the clouds right above. The weather is always mutable and at a moment's notice it can cycle through all four seasons. Winters are particularly brutal and unforgiving – harsh winds chill to the bone, relentlessly whip the unfortunate travelers and crack their lips the instant they set foot outside.

It was snowing heavily the entire week and the cold was mind-numbing. I went out to pick up groceries and I rushed to get back to my apartment as fast as possible. All I could think about was how to make the next step through the snow that creaked rhythmically beneath my feet. *Creak*

creak – whimper – creak creak – whimper. I stopped and listened. A faint cry originated from the cardboard box near the dumpster. I looked in it and, under a bunch of old newspapers, found a small puppy, unable to shiver any more than he was already. When I approached, he tried to look at me but couldn't raise his head due to how violently he was shaking. I instantly realized the situation – I was this puppy's last chance. He was already dying. I had to do something.

Without thinking, I took the puppy out of the box, put him underneath my left armpit, where my body is the warmest, and squeezed him tightly. Immediately upon feeling my body heat, he calmed down.

I entered my building, distracted the superintendent with small talk about the weather, and snuck the puppy into my apartment. Once inside, I found an old shoebox, lined it with towels and tucked him in. Only then could I take a better look. He was around three weeks old, with completely black fur marked by a white streak going down his belly. I figured out a name for him: Jooxie. I turned up the heating and went about my normal daily routine, knowing that it wouldn't be long until I saw activity from Jooxie. And soon enough, from the corner of my eye I noticed the towels move, and a tiny black tail emerged and started vigorously wagging. A small nose soon followed, then a set of curious eyes. In the next half an hour, Jooxie was out of the box and jumping merrily around, peeking into every corner.

Even though he had been on the brink of death just a while before, Jooxie didn't seem to be bothered by that at all. He was alive, bristling with energy. As I watched him explore and run around, I thought about how animals live with no regrets. We humans, on the other hand, seem to be unable to escape them. I was about to add another regret to my list. The fact of the matter was that I could not keep Jooxie. He was going to be discovered sooner or later. The terms of my lease clearly stated that pets weren't allowed and although technically Jooxie wasn't my pet, I doubted that the superintendent or the landlord would appreciate the finer points of my argument.

Three days passed and Jooxie recovered completely. I fed him abundantly and I was pleased to see his little tummy rounded. It was breaking my heart, but I had to let him go. I snuck him back out and, just letting his nose peek through my coat, I stopped people on the street and asked them if they would be willing to accept Jooxie into their home. Most of them outright refused, but I wasn't willing to give up. Finally, an older man showed interest. I let Jooxie out and he instantly bonded with the man and started licking his face. The man was surprised with such affection and laughed like a child. I knew at that moment everything was going to be alright. I shook the man's hand and we separated.

Life sometimes connects us through such situations which change us in completely unexpected ways. At first, I was sorry for giving Jooxie away, but as I remembered the jolly patter of his tiny paws on the floor of my apartment, a sudden wave of serenity overwhelmed me. I realized I shouldn't feel regret. All those moments with Jooxie will forever stay with me and I will remember them with fondness. Because of this little puppy, I learned that it is necessary to give without asking or expecting a reward and in return we receive far more than we ever hoped for.

About the Author
Dejan Savanovic has always had a keen eye for details. With age, his perception increased and his perspective changed to the point of realization that he is a part of an immense tapestry of human lives connected through what we're told are ordinary daily events. Dejan writes because he firmly believes that he can inspire others and add to the endless flow of thoughts, emotions and ideas we all create by sharing with each other, which enriches our lives beyond our wildest imagination.

How My Daddy Taught Me How to Be Kind
By Sheila Salyers, West Virginia, USA

"But Daddy, WHAT does the PAPER say!" I whined. "We passed by too fast for me to read it."

"Eat your lunch," Daddy said, gazing out the window at the man who was standing on the median.

Crossing my arms and putting on my very best "I will NOT" pout, I looked at my daddy and raised my eight-year-old chin to show him how serious I was, that I was NOT going to eat until he answered my question.

Sighing deeply, he looked down at his only child and shook his head. "If you eat, I'll tell you what the sign says."

Grinning, knowing I had won, I crammed my chicken chunks and fries in my mouth.

"Don't choke yourself silly, girl, or you'll die not knowing." Daddy smiled at me lovingly.

Thinking of this, I slowed down and began chewing more carefully – there was no way I could die not knowing, why, that would kill me! Between bites, I kept glancing out the fast food restaurant window at the man. He wore ragged pants with holes in them, and dirt seemed to be caked on him as if it were some kind of odd shirt. I had never seen anyone so dirty in my entire, whole eight-year-old life!

Finishing my last fry, I made a big production of wadding up the paper and throwing it on the tray. Daddy smiled at me and said, "Good girl, are you ready to go see Mommy?"

"I am not moving until you keep your word," I said in my "I am not giving in" voice.

"Sheila..." he began, and I crossed my arms and stuck out my lip.

I interrupted, "You promised!"

"I did no such thing," Daddy countered.

"But you said you would and I did not think you would lie to me, Daddy."

"Oh good grief child, why are you so curious?"

"Because that is the way I was made," I said.

"Come sit beside me," Daddy said, and I made my way over in a very unladylike fashion, crossed arms, pouted lips and all. "Let me start by telling you, baby girl, that not all people in life are as fortunate as you are. You never have to worry about having food to eat, or a nice warm bed, right?"

"Well I don't know about that, Daddy, I thought I was going to starve before you finally stopped here and got me food."

"Ugh, you were hungry for FIVE minutes before we stopped."

"What does any of this have to do with the man, Daddy?"

Rubbing my hair, my daddy pulled me closer and said, "The sign says, Will Work for Food."

Looking confused, eyebrows creased, I asked what THAT meant.

"Well, it looks like he may not have a job, and he is hungry and he is willing to do odd jobs to get some food to eat."

Stricken, I turned around and looked at my father. "Daddy, why does he not just come in here and get some food."

"Because he has no money, sweetheart."

"But Daddy, if he has no money, and he has no food, how is going to eat and not be hungry?"

Taking a very deep breath, Daddy looked at me and said, "I don't know."

"But Daddy, we can't let him go hungry." My lip quivered as my eyes filled with tears and I looked up at the man I knew could fix anything.

"Baby, we cannot give him money, we don't know if he is being honest."

Tears falling down my cheeks, I asked innocently, "What do you mean, Daddy?"

"Oh baby, why must you ask so many questions?" Daddy reached down and kissed my forehead, "Okay, some people will go out and stand like that, with signs, hoping people will give them money and then they go and buy beer with that money. We don't want to help with that by accident."

Crying steadily now, I looked my daddy in the eyes and said, "Daddy, we can't just let him be hungry."

Turning from his distraught daughter, Daddy looked at the man on the median. He was thinking I could tell. "Okay, we will do something, you believe and trust me."

"Yes, Daddy, of course," I replied.

"Get in the car, we're going to the store." Daddy smiled his best smile, the one that meant that we had a mission that only we knew about.

Going to a different part of the parking lot, we got out and went into the grocery store. There might as well have been two kids instead of one little girl and her daddy as we picked up a loaf of bread, pack of bologna, and a carton of milk, and of course a chocolate snack cake because every good meal needed dessert. Leaving the store, we were giggling, both happy that we were going to help someone!

Daddy slowed the car down as we approached the median, and the man turned and looked at us. He was older, I could see at this distance, deep wrinkles drawn into his face. Daddy handed the bag to him from the window and as the man approached the car, he looked as if Daddy was handing him a million dollars, looking in the bag, his eyes filled up with tears. Daddy put the car in drive and started to pull away.

"Wait!" the man cried out. "Thank you for your kindness. I have been here all day, and you are the first person to stop."

My daddy choked back his tears as he said, "Don't thank me, thank her," as he pointed over to me.

Suddenly shy, I dropped my head as the man looked at me and whispered, "Thank you." I smiled as much as I could and as Daddy pulled away, I whirled around in the seat to watch as the man sat down, opened his bag and started making himself a sandwich.

Years later I found out that my father had used his very last five dollars to buy that meal for a stranger. I will never forget the look on the stranger's face, nor the look of, what I now realize, was pride on my daddy's face as he ruffled my hair and said, "I sure do love you."

About the Author:
Sheila Salyers is a paralegal and freelance writer. Sheila has been writing since the age of eleven when she wrote her first poem. Currently living in Bluefield, West Virginia, with her husband, Sheila is now working on her first novel now that both of her children are raised.

Figure 11. Sheila and Dad years later

Jadika's Plight
By Timothy Munene, Kenya

The evening sun half dips on the horizon, sending crimson rays across the tin roofs of crowded abodes. In the space between squeezed shanties, a frenzy of activity occurs as womenfolk try to take advantage of the slipping daylight to cook. Work goes along with talk. There is much chatter as the women go about preparing the most important meal of the day. From the little girls to the old grandmas, this is the time when all proudly apply their skills. No respectable woman would want to be left out.

At the edge of this frenzy, sitting under an awning of one tin roof, dark round eyes peek through the fading light, dejectedly gazing at the women as they go about their duties. A closer look into the shadows reveals that the eyes belong to a young woman left out.

"Jadika! Where is the water I sent you for?" a buxom woman shouts.

"You didn't..." the young girl starts to reply but thinks better of it. Slowly, she rises from the log, where she had etched some respite, albeit only for a few minutes. With a forlorn look, she drags her weary feet to an empty plastic water container that lies on a muddy patch nearby. To her, this seems to be the umpteenth time she has gone down to

the solitary water tap that provides water for the whole community.

Jadika can cook; in fact, she is very good when it comes to culinary skills. However, she is wary of joining the others. They all know her story... Would they let her join them?

Quite tall for a girl let alone one at twelve years of age, Jadika's maturity seems to have come earlier. Her eyes tell stories, suggesting being forced to adapt to circumstances beyond her control.

Several years prior, Jadika had been one of the happiest and most adored girls in this neighborhood. She skipped around the sorry structures, home to many, ingenuously unaware of the poverty that surrounded her. Often she went along whistling a song. Many girls would look at her with envy, as she sucked on a ball of hard-boiled sweet syrup stuck on a stick, which she unknowingly teased the others with as she flicked her tongue around the colorful sweetness. She was better off than her peers; her mother and father never seemed to run out of money and gifts for her.

They said her only concern back then was that she often had to sleep alone at night in their small house. Her parents often went out at night. Many times they would come home drunk in the wee hours of the morning. Despite this, they always seemed to have something for their beautiful daughter.

Jadika's mother was the first to fall sick. Her father became withdrawn and seemed to drink even more. At the age of ten, Jadika took it upon herself to do all she could to bring her mother back to normal. No one else seemed to care or be able to help. Unfortunately, her mother only seemed to get worse. Jadika's own health deteriorated as she sat day and night beside her ailing mother. When her mother eventually succumbed to the illness and died, the young girl blamed herself.

As it is with many girls, Jadika loved her father very much. Her father adored her as well. After her mother's death, their bond became tighter. Her father drank more often and was often remorseful and withdrawn, but Jadika always seemed to lift his spirits with her presence. He was clearly deteriorating in health, but he was always in high spirits when he went walking along the street with his daughter. Jadika was showered with gifts and it seemed to drive a pike into the hearts of the other girls around the community who could never dream of such luxuries as she received.

Jadika's father continued his night activities, from which he seemed to get his money. After some time, however, he was overcome with sickness and he could not leave the house. Jadika was forced to repeat her nursing ordeal; this time however, it was short-lived... her father seemed to want to free his loving daughter from the hardship his handicap presented.

More than five months after Jadika became an orphan, a lot happened. As quickly as she was admired, she became a pariah in the community. As it is in such a community, word spreads fast. It had become apparent to many that Jadika's parents had contracted "the disease". With the kind of lifestyle they lived, no one would offer them a helping hand when they got sick. Perhaps Jadika did not know then why no one would help. She may have thought it was because they were a minority. Whatever their judgment, she faced the end result. The ghetto is not forgiving; after her parents' death, she was often openly accused of her parents' "sins", and many shunned her, believing that she also carried "the disease".

After her father's death, Jadika managed to survive on some money that he left behind for her, and she was taken in by one of her mother's friends. Eventually, Jadika stopped going to school. Although it is free to attend, school proved to be too tormenting for her. In the past, Jadika had been a prom queen among maids; after her parents' deaths, she did not have a single friend. The boys gave her wide berth; the men shot her accusing glares. The women told their children to stay away from her. The girls gave her hell. Soon the money that her father had left behind dwindled. Even her guardian started mistreating her and using her for all kinds of cheap labor... It seemed like this would continue without end.

Recently, I visited Jadika's home area and I was shocked to see a turn of events. She had become integrated in the community, once again, interacting with people in the neighborhood. What could have happened after such a short time to bring this change? I came to learn that Jadika's aunt was responsible.

The aunt lived close by. Quite successful in her own separate business, she had not related very well to Jadika's parents and had kept distance from them. However, when she saw how much Jadika was suffering, she took Jadika in and realized that the only way that Jadika was going to have a normal life was if the community accepted her.

Using her influence, Jadika's aunt invited several organizations into the area to help teach people about AIDs. The community was also educated to understand that even if a person is infected with AIDs, they should not be segregated and that they should be loved. Fortunately, Jadika had not contracted the virus from her parents. Although many are still skeptical about Jadika and others like her, many are now more accommodating.

Understandably, to this day, Jadika is still traumatized and guarded about the people around her. She has gone through a lot. To bring her out of her cocoon, the community tries to involve her in their daily activities. They have reached out.   All it took was one person to make a difference.

"After you bring the water, come, let's share these oranges I brought from the market," the alto voice continues. Lifting the empty container from the muddy patch, a shy smile faintly appears to touch the tall skinny girl's lips.

About the Author:

Timothy Munene is a writer based in Kenya who has authored many creative articles with an African theme. Holding a bachelors degree in IT, he is often involved in charity work in IT for NGOs working for the benefit of the less fortunate in Kenya.

Lessons Learnt
By Karan Sampat, India

"Karan, please finish your lunch. This is the third time this week you haven't finished your lunch."

"I don't like it, Ma'am."

"Then tell your mother to send something you like."

"She doesn't listen at all."

"I will talk to her at the next parent-teacher meeting."

With that, the teacher went off to manage the other kids, as I slowly slid my lunch back into my bag. I was hungry, but my dislike for the food went deep so I decided to not eat. The next three hours of school were a blur, with my stomach groaning and grumbling. But, my stubbornness to not eat the salad remained resolute. It was a matter of principle.

When the bell rang to signal that it was time for us to head home, I was the first through the door. My pace slowed to a crawl as my empty stomach denied me the strength to run. Clutching my belly, I trudged through the long kilometer which separated home from school. Cars raced past me on the road, and I wished I had been in one of them. Unfortunately, our car's tire had gotten punctured earlier this morning.

With a sigh and a shake of my head, I kept moving forward. Sleep and hunger mixed to create a dangerous cocktail of emotions within me. A thought occurred to me as I stopped dead in my tracks.

"Today the driver isn't there to eat my lunch. If Mother learns that I haven't eaten my lunch, she will shout and will make me finish it in front of her!!!" I panicked.

"This is such a big problem." I said to myself.

"I can't throw it away. That's a waste." I was practically sobbing. My punishment was imminent.

My eyes shifted nervously everywhere, suddenly afraid of all the shadows, thinking that my mother would materialize from somewhere and make me eat the salad I hated. Oh, the terror!

At that moment, in the distance, something caught my eye. I moved closer to have a look. There sat a family, dressed in tattered rags, as thin as sticks, and dirty from not having a bath in who knows how long. Wrinkling my nose, I watched as one of them pulled out a small plastic bag from inside his pocket... All of their eyes widened in happiness as it contained some small food.

Admittedly, the idea that came to me first was one of self-interest. I thought of escaping punishment by offering them my detestable salad. It was a win-win situation.

I pulled my packed greens out of my bag and walked to the thinnest child and handed the box to him. The look on his face was a mix of wonder and bliss, and when I nodded and opened the box for him, his smile widened. The smile on his face stretched from ear to ear and he looked for a minute from me to the box and then to his family. He tried to say something, but words were failing him, so I said, "Go on and eat."

Barely managing a thank you, he went off to gobble down what I had not eaten due to choice. After two mouthfuls, he turned to his family, and offered it to them all, and however hungry they were, they denied his offer, giving him the luxury of a meal alone. Not only this, the boy went to the other destitute families and passed my lunchbox around.

The smiles on all the faces were blissful, and as the kid handed me the box back and I began walking, the kid's mother called out to me and said, "Sir, thank you. May God bless you."

I was stunned.

I just smiled and began walking in the direction of home. This simple act had made such a difference to them. The hunger in my stomach ceased to bother me. Somehow watching this scene, I felt happy too. The small idea of giving my lunch away to the kid had turned from a necessity to an act of kindness. This deed had made me feel better as a person.

I had managed to fill an empty stomach, and I was even blessed by them for it. Along with this, I had learnt another thing and that was what it means to share. With an empty stomach and food in hand, the kid had turned to share with his family and the people with him. He did not enjoy it all alone.

As I entered my house, I realized though I probably would never like salads I could appreciate them more. Also, I resolved to bring back and give treats to the kids in the neighborhood. To give is the greatest gift of all.

About the Author:
Karan Sampat is a young writer who loves to read and experiment with different styles of writing. One of his goals in life is to spread the light of knowledge.

Lost In Peru

By Grace Chen, Pennsylvania, USA

It *had* seemed like a good idea at the time… With my blurry vision, I squinted groggily at the billboards and unfamiliar brown faces. Damn, myopia! I couldn't see a thing. Of course, I should have gotten a new prescription before jet-setting across the globe, but this trip had happened so quickly. I'd gotten on the plane faster and more determined than I had allowed myself time to reflect on the potential flaws of my grand design.

Families hugged each other. Friends embraced. The indistinct outlines of traffic bustled past me. I tugged my heavy suitcase – the only thing I was familiar with there – closer behind me. It weighed too little to offer much comfort. It was up to me and me alone to rally my spirits. Peru is a safe, fun-loving country. It's not scary. Not scary at all. Not knowing Spanish is not a problem. Random women disappearing on holiday trips?

Ha, can't imagine how that could happen.

Jetlag was disorienting, but nothing I couldn't shake off – with a little emergency adrenaline! In fact, my healthy discomfort with unfamiliar situations might be useful in keeping me awake long enough to find a guide.

Come on, guide! I paid you lots of money. Where are you?

I scanned the crowd again for some kind of recognition. I looked at my watch. I scanned the crowd again. I looked at my watch. Repeat. Repeat. Repeat. *Ad infinitum.*

Would anyone make eye contact with me? *No, not you sir, not in a creepy way. No ma'am, I don't mean to pick a fight. I just am looking for help… Someone… Someone…*

My heart began to sink as I remembered how late at night it was. My flight had incurred unexpected delays. I was supposed to arrive at ten p.m. It was now two a.m. *Would a courtesy shuttle be courteous enough to wait four hours past due?*

Vaguely, I remember I had wanted to teach myself to be brave. Flying to a foreign country on my own seemed like such a big step. I would be leaving the confines of parental control. It would be one more step towards freedom.

You have to gradually crawl before you can run, right?

Quickly, I pulled out my "EZ Spanish" guidebook from my backpack; it promised to teach me important phrases within twenty-four hours or less. Maybe there was some useful saying in here? *Where is the police station?* Yet, there didn't seem to be a phrase for "lost and scared." It was so very late at night.

Suddenly, a chill crept over me. My goose bumps propped up the fine pale hairs on my forearms.

How long could I stand here like this? It had been over an hour. Literally, it was now three a.m.

Soon, I began to worry in earnest. Would this be a huge disaster? I might not be kidnapped, but how stupid would it be to be trapped in an airport for the duration of my four-day trip.

Next to me, a man was on the phone, speaking in half-English and half-Spanish. He saw me staring frantically. When he was done, he hung up. I thought he was going to admonish me for listening in. I blurted out first, "Do you speak English?" *Please. Please. Please. Speak English.* "Habla Anglos?"

Nodding his head, he said "yes." He had a kind look on his face.

Encouraged, I asked, "Do you know how to get a taxi?"

Worry filled his soft brown eyes.

"Are you alone?"

Hesitating for a bit since this was a total stranger, I finally answered in a long-winded fashion, "Yes, but there is someone waiting for me. They are supposed to be here. They'll know where I am." It was probably more explanation than he needed.

"Really, is there?"

My eyes started to dart around. "I think so..."

His eyes grew rounder and wider, filling with concerns.

He called his friend back and told them that they would have to wait.

For the next half-hour, this total stranger waited with me. He helped me find my tour guide. I never got his name, but to this day I remember how concerned he was for my safety. Since then, of course, I have travelled quite a bit more and am more prepared on my adventures. Though I am older, I still think back on this. How nice must a person be to take that long bit of time out of their day – at three in the morning – to wait with a total stranger? I would like to be able to say no small deed is ever forgotten. Next time I have the opportunity, I am going to make sure to pay it forward. You never know how much help a person might need or what kind of impact it will make on them.

About the Author:
Grace Chen is a scientist. Her hobbies include reading, writing, cooking, and jujitsu. She is trying to be more adventurous. Soon, she will travel to Japan.

Figure 12. Actual Photo from Peru

Meeting God's Own Child
By Shruti Fatehpuria, India

I distinctly remember one of the incidents that occurred when I was vacationing in Bhutan. Bhutan – the Himalayan kingdom – has given me too many fond memories; it is a place after my own heart. However, here I will share a tale that made me ponder life from a different perspective.

I remember throwing temper tantrums at my mother because she refused to let me buy my favorite clothes. Bhutan isn't home to the fanciest shops, so when I found a really great dress, I so badly wanted to have it. However, when she told me that it wasn't worth the money, I started sulking.

Yet, she was the elder there, and I was the one with no power whatsoever in the matter. So, off we went for our trekking trip. As we were walking on the meandering lanes, I found a little girl sitting on the banks of a stream, smiling to herself.

Her face was radiating happiness and if I had been an artist, I would have loved to sketch the beautiful happiness that radiated from her face. We waved at her and she smiled back and waved. It was common for people in Bhutan to talk to random strangers and this girl was no different. She came up to us and started telling us about how wonderful it is to live her life in this Himalayan kingdom.

She told us many stories, and every single one of them spoke about her happiness. I thought she was one of the luckiest girls alive and God had gifted her so much to be thankful and happy for. She smiled when I told her so, and she invited us over to her home for tea and snacks.

As we approached, I saw that the home she was talking about was just a small room with barely space for two. There were five of them who lived there, and she cheerily called out her uncle and aunt to introduce us.

I later asked where her parents were and she smiled and said, "They are my parents. I am lucky. God took away my parents because he loved them, but he made sure I had my uncle and aunt who loved me equally, if not more." Then she looked at them and smiled and my heart warmed all over again.

She must not have been over ten years old, but her deep insight into the world made me wonder at her in amazement. Her uncle then told us about how hard it is to make a living because there aren't huge employment opportunities, and feeding a big family with three children can be a demanding job, but he was sure this is all God's plan and He will see them through.

The girl in particular was the one who stayed on my mind. Seeing her happy face, no one could ever imagine that she was an orphan and her family was struggling to make both ends meet. Now that I knew her story, I looked at her and saw that her little pink dress was dirty. It had faded and there were dirt marks all over it.

Such was her happy face that I had failed to notice all of it. Instantly, I recalled how I had been throwing my temper tantrums at my mother for not allowing me to buy a top, and right here in front of me was a girl – an orphan, a poor girl with barely any money, and yet she exemplified the epitome of happiness.

My heart pricked at the thoughts and I realized one of the biggest lessons there is. Happiness is a decision that we have the power to make. You can choose to be happy or sad – it is entirely your own call. I went back to my hotel room and took out one of the several new dresses that I had. I came back to the little happy girl and gifted it to her because it seemed pointless to have so many.

As I gave her the dress, she was touched. She smiled the kind of angelic smile that melted my heart. She thanked me innumerable times because it had been so long since she had bought anything so fancy. Perhaps she had never bought anything so fancy in her whole life. I gave her my email address and I urged her to stay in touch.

The little girl looked every bit like an angel visiting from heaven who comes in your life to teach you some important lessons. I shared my email address, but in my heart, I knew that we would probably never see each other again because the internet in Bhutan wasn't the most accessible resource. For someone who could barely make ends meet, using the internet seemed out of the question. Yet, one could hope, and so I did. We finally exchanged our greetings and departed their home.

I left Bhutan with some of the best memories and the hope that life might bring the two of us together again. Three weeks after returning back from Bhutan when I received an email from an unknown address.

I opened the email and I was too stunned to speak. It was an email from the little girl with an attachment that showed her in the same dress I had gifted her. She was radiating happiness and she emailed me, "Thank you for gifting me a gift I would have never got otherwise. This is not just a dress but a token of love for me. I have been trying hard to send this to you, but it was hard to get an internet connection. I hope you will see this and feel happy too."

There is no way to count the number of times I read that email. Sometimes, happiness happens.

It was just another dress for me, but for that little girl, it was a gesture of friendship, a token of love, an event that she will recall forever, and I learnt that life is more than fretting over little things. It is a journey which is meant to cherish every small and big thing that brings you joy.

About the Author:

A misfit software engineer, Shruti Fatehpuria left work in the corporate world to pursue her dream. Her passion lies in talking of things she relates to, and living the stories she often dreams of. Born in India, Shruti grew up with too many fairy tales and fancies living a life that turns out to be a story that can inspire others. She is on a voyage where she is in pursuit of herself, and she is sure that reality and her dreams will one day collide.

Figure 13. Between the mountains of Bhutan

No Ice Cream for Dad
By Darcy Sprague, Texas, USA

My dad is my favorite person and my hero. He is one of those characters that normally only exists in books or movies. Strong, Selfless, and a retired soldier, he is still supporting his family today, at the age of fifty-nine.

It was a Sunday night, I was about six, and my dad was finally home from work. Ever since I was a baby, my dad would randomly take me out for a treat a couple of nights a week, and that night he decided to take me to Dairy Queen. I was ecstatic about the idea of ice cream, but I was more excited just to spend time with him.

My dad's favorite ice cream dish has always been a root beer float. He was absolutely obsessed with them. He ordered a large while I order some overly expensive, complicated-named chocolate dish. One of those that have so many ingredients you can barely eat a small portion before you feel queasy. The grand total for the two of us was about twelve dollars, but my dad had only brought a ten. I knew enough about money to be sad and a little embarrassed that we didn't have enough money for our order, even though I knew he had more at home. My dad apologized and asked to change his to a medium. It was still over ten dollars. He asked to change it to a small, and then to cancel his altogether. Never once did he ask me to downsize mine, even though I had taken advantage of my mom's absence and ordered an ice cream way too large for me. When I did offer to change mine to just an ice cream cone, he waved me off.

In the end the lady at the register offered to pay the difference and my dad and I ate our ice cream. In the car on the way home, I asked my dad if we had to drive back to Dairy Queen and give the lady the change that we were short, which ended up being about fifty cents. He said no, that good people do small things to help each other every day, and their reward is that one day they will need someone else to do something for them, and they will.

I felt special when my dad sacrificed most of his portion for me, but no matter how hard I tried, I could not finish my dish. He told me that he remembers having to bring me cups of warm water because I kept getting a headache. It was selfish of me to order that much, even though I didn't know better at the time.

It was such a simple day, but my dad's willingness to sacrifice something he wanted completely, so that I didn't have to give up a thing I didn't need, has always had a large impact on me. It taught me two lessons; that giving, in some way, to help someone else, makes them feel really good, and not to take more than you need.

Now I am preparing to go to college, and my dad is still sacrificing everything he can to help me get what I want. I love him. He is truly the best human being I have ever known.

About the Author:

Darcy Sprague and her mother wrote her first story when she was too young to put the words on paper herself. Ever since then, writing has been her passion and escape. She never had a solid answer for what she wanted to be as she grew up, but her junior year English teacher inspired her to start writing more. Currently, Darcy attends Texas State University and is majoring in journalism. She hopes to one day be working on exciting and danger-filled stories. Her ultimate goal is to publish a novel.

Figure 14. Piggy-back rides courtesy of my Dad

The Old Lady and the Orange
By R. Gonzales, Philippines

I do not know how she knew it was me. I don't know how she still remembered when she was so old. Could it be because she truly had some supernatural powers?

She was a thin, tall woman with a stooped back. Whenever she smiled or talked, her words came out shaken and prolonged, like a snake hissing in vibrato. But what I probably would remember best was that she had orange teeth and orange drool.

"Pests! Pests! Oh, what pestilence!" she would shout at us, scrambling out from her shabby little house. No, "house" is too fancy a word. She lived in a four-square-meter of plastic, scrap wood, some bamboo and coconut leaves. The children would scamper away in screams of part-fright and part-laughter.

To a child of seven or eight, she was a witch. But children would gather near her fence every afternoon when classes and nap times were over and parents had become lenient because it would also be their time to engage in neighborly conversations (more like gossip). It was so because the herbs growing in her front yard were those that possessed magical properties such as dyeing skins purple, and creating bubbles.

I was trying to sneak into her yard to collect some bubble-making herbs (they're real! they're magical!) one afternoon, when she suddenly popped out from nowhere and cornered me.

"Where's your father?" she hissed from between her discolored, crooked, and wide-spaced teeth.

"I don't know," I said, unable to run away because I thought it would be rude and because her orange teeth were all too fascinating, even as they were revolting.

"You have pretty eyes," she said.

I blinked, focusing on her mouth. I was almost tempted to say she had pretty hair or pretty teeth or pretty anything. But I had been taught that lying was bad.

"Would you like some bread?"

I blinked back. I shook my head.

"Come, come."

I followed her to the opening of her house. Where the door should be was only a drape of cloth. There were three or four steps of bamboo ladder to her shack. I did not climb up with her.

She handed out a piece of bread which I so reluctantly but politely took a bite of. I knew children were not supposed to take anything from strangers, but she was not entirely a stranger. The whole neighborhood knew her and the shack was in plain sight of the other houses. Besides, I did not want to offend a witch. Never mind that I imagined the bread to be moldy. Baked in an oven of creepy crawly things or something. Surprisingly, it tasted normal.

One day, a tall tree near our house bore orange nut-like fruits. From a reliable adult, I came to know that it was a betel nut tree. Chewing its nuts, they said, makes old people (from our part of the world) happy. I did not entirely believe it, but I stopped asking.

Was I trying to make friends with her? Did I want to return the kindness she showed me? Perhaps. I harassed (in a most endearing, childish way) a grown-up to get me those attractive orange nuts so I could pack them inside a plastic bag and very quietly leave them by the old woman's front door.

Within that year of our encounter, my parents decided to move much closer to the city. Occasionally, the poor woman would walk right through my mind in a wobbly gait. Shamefully, I couldn't invite her to stay because school and other mundane stuff took up much of the space. And she'd walk right out, so serenely.

Many years later, I returned to the scene of my childhood for a visit – the place with grassy vacant lots, interesting trees and stooped, stained-teeth women. I was almost eighteen at the time. The old woman was still there in her makeshift house. More hunched than ever and now with cloudy eyes, she managed to outlive many people I personally knew, including my mother. No longer did she seem a witch. Only a very old and frail, forgotten daughter, sister, or mother of somebody – and perhaps that's how I saw her when I left that small package by her house.

"I won't forget how you left me those betel nuts. I won't forget," she said to me casually. It was the same shaking, hissing voice – only quieter.

I was taken aback.

She'd said that to me as a child when my act was discovered (within that same week, I guess). She had thanked me with eyes that shone with what I, even as a child, could identify as pride and joy. But as an adult? I couldn't believe she still remembered! I couldn't believe how happiness could still shine from her eyes at something that happened so long ago.

I will never forget how she mentioned it through toothless, orange smiles and moist eyes in the liveliest tones she could muster. Not a sports car, not a diamond. Only three orange betel nuts she could consume in one day. Most of all, it had been years and years!

And actually, I also remember her "moldy" bread. I clearly do. Though ordinary and old, it was most probably all she had that afternoon. In hindsight, it was her simple act of kindness that precipitated mine.

Sometimes I still wonder how she knew it was me who left her the betel nuts. Was keen memory part of her witchcraft? Or is it because when kindness starts singing, whether through a child or an old woman, its soothing voice echoes through eternity?

About the Author:
R. Gonzales is a spectator of the universe. Whatever she finds beautiful and worthwhile, she struggles to preserve through the pen. She currently lives in a seaside town in the Philippines.

One Golden Sun

By Tammisan Mason, California, USA

One of the most magical and memorable boat rides any child can take is the one that gently floats on the waters of Walt Disney's "Small World" ride. The tiny vessel begins the enchanting journey by entering a tunnel beneath bright white arches trimmed in generously applied sparkly gold. For fifteen entire minutes there is nothing but total immersion in a world of color, unity, and a sense of peace. The welcome room is alive with greetings offered by festively costumed dolls from across the globe, presenting the rider a chance to see native dress, dance and customs from around the world. Each set of geographical dolls sing in a different language, and surprisingly, they all are in harmony, gracefully timed to the same melody.

Written for Disney's attraction at the 1964 World's Fair, that song is the only work ever to be granted public domain status by Walt Disney. The proceeds from the ride went to UNICEF, who had requested that Disney not restrict the use of the theme song. The lack of cumbersome copyright mandates on the composition enabled children from all over the globe to sing, write, print and reproduce both music and lyrics. It was indeed a gift to the entire world.

It's a world of laughter, a world of tears
It's a world of hopes and a world of fears
There's so much that we share that it's time we're aware
It's a small world after all
It's a small world after all
It's a small world after all
It's a small world after all
It's a small, small world
There is just one moon and one golden sun.
And a smile means friendship to everyone.
Though the mountains divide,
And the oceans are wide
It's a small world after all.

As a child, it was my favorite ride at Disneyland's theme park; it was my mother's as well. I can still remember her humming and singing it on long car rides or while puttering around our house. I believe that somehow the song had long since been embroidered on both of our hearts. Time would tell.

&

A decade and a half after my first "Small World" boat ride, I was a student at the University of California's Santa

Barbara campus. To help with tuition and expenses, I had gotten a job at a local newspaper. Although my immediate supervisor was planning to leave for a new career in the cable industry, we made fast friends. It was the summer between my freshman and sophomore years that she called and offered me a one day mini-job; the compensation was remarkable and the work light. I accepted. However, her instructions on the appropriate attire required were rather curious: *"Just wear something over a bathing suit. And bring a towel."*

Sunglasses, tanning lotion, and towel in tow, I headed down to the center of Santa Barbara where her office was located. It was a Sunday morning and the sun was unusually hot for the coastal town. Before I knew it, we were off on an adventure – an adventure I would never forget. The destination: Bakersfield, California. Anyone who has lived in or visited Bakersfield in the summertime can attest to the fact that the heat can become so blazingly intense that an egg could be fried on the sidewalk. Literally. My former boss, Brin, had left *that* small detail off the job description, and with good reason. I had made a summer trip to Bakersfield in high school with a church group and had sworn I would never *ever* return; she just happened to know this. Growing up along the Southern California shoreline had spoiled me when it came to weather; 70 degrees with mild winds off the water suited me just fine.

We headed up for the mountainous trek leading to the high desert. The drive was absolutely breathtaking, with its large pines and fabulous rock formations. We passed hikers, bicycle enthusiasts, and sightseers snapping photos of the majestic beauty that surrounded us. Just as I was being lulled into pristine serenity, it happened: we hit the high desert. While it too can be beautiful, it is most beautiful from inside a car equipped with massive amounts of air conditioning. Well, that's my opinion at least. Mother Nature visually responded to the change in climate conditions by taking away all the lusciousness of the forest and replacing it with prickly bushes and miles of seemingly endless dirt. The prettiest things upon which to look were the marvelous California mountains trimming the horizon; and *they* were hundreds of miles away.

Brin explained what my duties were. The cable company she worked for was going to be opening up shop in Bakersfield. In order to inspire cable subscribers to choose their service over their competitor's, they were offering free viewings of blockbuster movies not yet released for purchase. What I heard next was unusual. One expects movies to be transmitted from some high-tech mixing studio; in this case they were not. They were being handled at a tiny little steel and concrete building on the very outskirts of town. What they needed was someone to man the controls, so to speak, and to put the right movies on at exactly the right time. I was told it would be a breeze. ("*Oh sure,*" I had thought, "*There **are no** worthwhile breezes in Bakersfield!*")

On the drive to the location where I would spend the next twelve hours, I was given a brief rundown of the situation. The movies and intermittent sales pitches I would be feeding into the system lasted up to four hours, and during that runtime I had no responsibilities. The hut rested on the middle of a concrete slab and was surrounded by a tall chain link fence with barbed wire at the very top. Brin suggested that I tan out on the slab between movies, as there was nothing else to do there. This was a time long before iPods, iPads, iPhones and all the rest of the amazing gizmos and gadgets we enjoy today. Portable computers had not hit the mainstream yet, either. It was "read a book" time, or nothing at all.

Being the committed student that I was (wink wink), I had in fact grabbed some coursework that I'd been putting off for a rainy day. (It never rains in California.) This made the job even more fortuitous; I would be stuck with nothing to do but my homework *and* I would be getting paid to do it! Wonderful!

&

It was a long dirt road that led to what I had humorously nicknamed "the shed." (Officially, it was referred to as a "head-in.") As we approached, I realized I was one lone soldier in the midst of a very wide desert. The nearest signs of civilization were about a quarter of a mile away, and it too was surrounded by a high chain link fence. Between the two parcels was nothing but sandy dirt and small cactus-like vegetation.

On the way to the head-in, we'd stopped to pick up an executive with the cable company, a man named Barry. Barry was to instruct me on how the equipment worked and the actual mechanics of doing the job. As I had been told, it was pretty simple stuff. Mercifully, the head-in had a commercial air unit; the media equipment had to be kept at a continuous cool temperature. I was content. As they were leaving Barry gave a few last-minute instructions like, "I'm locking the gate around the shed; there should be no reason for you to go anywhere and it will keep anyone from bothering you." We had picked up food, water and some sweets on the way out of town; I was set for the duration. "Oh!" he said as he poked his head back in the door. "If you do decide to tan, make sure you prop the door open, it automatically locks itself." He shut the door behind him and then it was "The Trio" – Me, Myself and I, settling down for a long summer's study.

&

About three hours into the job I began to get restless. I had eaten lunch and then studied organic chemistry to the point of mental exhaustion. Having just started a movie, I had nearly a four-hour block of time on my hands.

As much as I hated the heat, I decided to take a few minutes to lie in the sun; maybe I could catch some color while being on-the-clock. I took off my shorts and T-shirt and rubbed on some tanning oil. I grabbed a chair to prop open the incredibly heavy, metal door, thinking all the while that the place really reminded me of what an above-ground bomb shelter would have been like, if they'd ever made them.

The best place to tan was around the corner from the door, so I put my towel down there. Soon I realized the cement was too hot, so I grabbed a couple of chairs from inside. I sat on one and put my feet up on the other. It didn't take long for me to get thirsty (I had chosen not to bring out water bottles because they would heat up too quickly). A trip back in and I had my bottle of water. It went fast. Really fast. I got up and got another. That one went fast too! *"Okay,"* I thought, *"this is ridiculous. I'm drinking them too fast for them to get hot, why not just bring out a few?"* I walked into the head-in for a third time. On my way in I kicked the chair out of the way, thinking I needed the head-in to be as cool as possible. I sat for a few minutes on the cold cement floor; then I checked the equipment to see how long I had. The movie wouldn't end for quite some time, so I gathered my bottles to go outside.

It occurred to me that the chair had in fact been letting in a large amount of heat. To safeguard the technical equipment, I decided to use one of the small empty water bottles to keep the door open a crack – enough to get back inside but not enough to let in a lot of air.

Back on my two-chairs I began to get sleepy. The hot sun and a full belly of water were gently inviting me to sleep. Then I heard a noise; the noise of something closing. It wasn't a car door sound; it wasn't a house door slamming; but I knew it wasn't just *any* door.

To my horror I recognized the sound; it was the distinct sound of *a heavy metal door! A heavy metal door closing!* I was afraid to look. Surely the water bottle was strong enough to hold the door, wasn't it? The answer was traumatizing, it was "NO"; no, it was not strong enough to hold the door open. I was there, outside, in the middle of nowhere, in extreme heat.... *in a string bikini.*

I sat down on the nearby chair, dumbfounded. What in the world was I going to do? I was trapped in an environmental Dutch oven! It was hard to think with the heat, but I knew I had to do something quickly.

I kept telling myself to think like MacGyver, the star of one of my favorite television shows. MacGyver did the best with what he had – he could take a piece of twine and a piece of bubblegum and build an ark. What did I have? I had two chairs, a towel, and three empty water bottles (thank goodness I was sloppy and hadn't taken them inside!). I knew I couldn't sit there and wait eight hours for Brin to come get me; I would be scorched. I went to work smashing the water bottles down as flat as I could get them, not an easy task with flip-flops.

I decided I needed to get help, and the only way to do that was to climb the fence. I surveyed the height of the fence and figured it would take at least three long strides to make it to the top. I also realized that the hot fence would be extremely hard to hold onto, so my plan was to squash the bottles down enough to use them as a buffer for my hands; my feet would have to endure. I grabbed the chair and hoisted the towel up over the barbed wire and proceeded to painstakingly climb the fence.

As I was beginning to make my descent I realized that I had left my flip-flops on the other side. As any beach girl knew, sand could get very hot; I figured dirt would also. I brought the towel down and sat on it. I began to estimate how long it would take me to cross the great divide between the head-in and the houses across the lot. Now that I was intently surveying them, they looked like houses made for migrant farm workers. Great. I spoke only a few words in Spanish and most of them were items from the Taco Bell menu. Although the sun was still blazing, my future was looking pretty dark.

I used the towel to inch towards the small shacks, taking one baby step at a time, moving the towel, and then repeating. Suddenly I heard the sound of children's voices; I looked closer and I could see a small group of young boys pointing at me.

"*Oh great, a mirage!*" I mused. On second thought I realized I wasn't hot enough to be seeing things yet; there actually was a group of kids waving! I screamed and motioned for them to come to me. They climbed their fence immediately and started running the distance of the divide, straight towards me. I felt like the luckiest girl in the world! I was being rescued! As they drew closer and then eventually circled around me, I suddenly felt like I was Glinda, the Good Witch of the North, surrounded by Munchkins! Snow White also popped into mind with her Dwarfs; however, the big difference was that I was not attired in a beautiful white gown or a beautiful collared gown. *I was still in that string bikini. YIKES.*

Trying not to let that fact deter me from my mission to survive the day, I pointed to their houses and then to myself and then back and forth. They spoke no English and the only foreign language I'd ever studied was French. A lot of good that was going to do me! I did remember though, that they were both Romance languages and probably had similar words. The problem was, I couldn't even remember one single word in French; well, except the songs. Somehow belting out a raucous chorus of "Frere Jacques," "Au Clair de la Lune," or "Mon Petit Chou" just didn't seem like an appropriate thing to do. And so I stood there, looking into their sweet little faces. Some were covered in dust, but all of them were smiling. They exuded something I had rarely seen: pure happiness.

They spoke fervently amongst themselves and then took off their shoes. Acting quickly, they each put one shoe down, and then another, forming a single line of shoes. They pointed at me to walk on them. It was the most touching and kind act of which I had ever been the recipient. I began to giggle as I looked at those precious little boys leading the way to a safe harbor; I had my own army of little men! As we reached the fence surrounding their community they all took their shirts off and battled to see who would push theirs through the chain link so that I might comfortably climb to the other side.

As little gentlemen, they did not intend to follow behind me (the string bikini I imagine); instead they began climbing on links adjacent to mine.

As soon as my little crew had reassembled, they led me to one of their houses. I cannot imagine what went through the mind of the boy's mother who walked into her living room and found a 5'7" white female complete with golden blonde hair and blue eyes standing there talking to her son and his friends. Oh yes, and in a string bikini. In retrospect I am sure she pondered, *"Guess who's coming to dinner – American-style?"* but after a moment her eyes signaled acceptance as she listened to the little ones describe my plight. Immediately she served me water, and probably most importantly, she handed me an extremely large dress!

&

I learned rather quickly that they did not have a phone in their home. However, through hand signals and gestures, they told me a neighbor did. The only problem was they were not home. And so I spent one of the most memorable afternoons of my life. The barrier created by not sharing a language quickly dissipated. We laughed and ate and drank lots of water!

I had joined a Mexican dancing troupe in junior high school and I happened to be an exceptional dancer. Before I knew it we had the small family radio blasting and I was dancing as if someone had left the gate open! (Ironically, they hadn't!) Neighbors came to join in the festivities and the fun, and, I'm sure, to see the *weda* (slang for white female) performing dance moves to "Jarabe Tapatio" (The Mexican Hat Dance) while wearing a dress big enough for a tent!

By the time I used the phone and reached Brin, I was saddened the night had to come to an end. I had made many new friends, friends that reached out and helped someone with whom they couldn't communicate. The boys had freely and without hesitation offered their shoes and shirts, literally off their feet and backs. The adults in their little village of homes had welcomed the "white girl" with open arms. They fed me incredible homemade dishes and insisted that I join in the experience of happiness. Their kindness and graciousness has never been matched in my fifty-two years of living.

As I sat in the back seat of the car, driving home under the bright twinkling stars, a little tune came to mind. It was the song that I had learned as a young girl; the one that told of unity, kindness, brotherhood and love. For the first time I realized that the song proclaiming "It's a Small World" was true. It **was** true! And although the ride is found in "Fantasyland" at every single Disneyland location in the world, its precepts are not fantasy at all. The truth is that it truly is a small world in which we live. It's a place where there's just one moon and one golden sun, and "*a smile means friendship to everyone.*"

About the Author:

Tammisan Mason, J.D. is a graduate of the University of California at Santa Barbara with two Bachelor's Degrees;

one in Political Science and the other in Religion. Although she was awarded her Juris Doctorate in 2007, beyond a shadow of a doubt she feels her most valuable accomplishments are daughter, Christa Courtney, and son, Troy Michael.

Figure 15. Tammisan and sons

Pay It Forward
By Belle Evelyn, Canada

It was raining on the first day of my new job as an errand girl for a huge corporate company in central London. I was twenty years old, super excited and completely soaked. The building towered over me and I stood outside, shaking in my first-ever pair of patent leather high heels.

It was a complete stroke of luck that I got the job – I was lucky enough to have some contacts through my aunt's friend's husband. I had learnt that that is how it works to get anywhere in the corporate industry; it's not who you are, it's who you know. Getting places is not a matter of being skilled and accomplished – although that helps; it is more about networking, knowing the right people.

Luckily, I managed to get myself this very small and insignificant job at a ginormous Fortune 500 company. One step at a time, I had to tell myself. I had to swallow a lot of pride to take the job – I was used to being the top of my class in high school and college and the president of a bunch of student organizations, so falling right back down to the bottom of the pile was about to be a real challenge.

I approached the building – it was my first time commuting to the center of London since work experience at age sixteen, and I was out of breath and sweating... not to mention drenched by the typical English rain. I went through the looming revolving door and was met with a very cold stare from the receptionist. The look on her face was compelling. We stared into each other's eyes for what felt like an hour. I finally remembered but had barely uttered the first syllable before he grumbled "fifth floor" and went back to texting.

I reached the fifth floor and looked through a pair of glass doors. Everything was wild and unstoppable; people were moving, running, shouting, waving. More people were perched on desks or dashing between them than sitting behind them in a chair. The lively atmosphere excited me but at the same time everyone looked completely unapproachable and very unfriendly.

I came from a deprived area of London and so I was here with the dreams of thousands of my peers on my back. Most of them would never dream of making it this far and so I had to do it for them. I had to prove that it was possible to climb the ladder of a huge company and make it big all by yourself. I had to prove that The Dream was not exclusive to Americans.

I walked into the giant, bustling office, and attempted to find my way to the manager's office. Along the way I received nothing but huffs of discouragement, evil glares, or shoves out of the way. My nerves increased – was this really going to be as good as I imagined? Just as I was turning the corner, a man came rushing round with a coffee and a pile papers which proceeded to fly into the air as we collided. The coffee came down half all over my brand new white shirt and half over his super-important legal documents. I was on the floor dazed and soaked in both rain and coffee, on the brink of tears as the man proceeded to fire expletives at me and march off, angrily. I took a deep breath and got up, pretty certain that I had also twisted an ankle; I carried on down the corridor followed by looks of disdain rather than sympathy...

The day was going absolutely terribly! I reached the manager's office and went in. He didn't even look up from his desk; he just gave me a list of instructions and asked for three donuts and a hot chocolate. I obliged and spent the day delivering coffee and food to miserable people who didn't say thank you or even look up from what they were doing. One step at a time, I kept reminding myself.

By the end of the week, I was exhausted and convinced that I couldn't do another day of being a neglected servant for a bunch of aggressive and rude bankers. I told myself that Friday would be my last day; I would walk away from that place and call it a learning experience to be remembered. I would much rather work at McDonald's, I thought; at least, there people interact with you.

On Friday morning, I came to work, stopping on the way for the manager's hot chocolate and coffee for several other people on ego trips.

On my desk I expected to find a long list of mundane and tiring jobs to do. Instead, I found a nice hot cup of tea and a note that read "you're doing a great job!"

I couldn't believe it… there must have been a mistake! I double-checked that I was in the right cubicle and sure enough, I was. Was this really for me? Maybe I had a secret admirer or maybe someone had finally noticed how hard I'd been working?! I finished the day with a smile still on my face.

On Monday, I returned and on my desk was a cookie and a book called *How to Survive as an Errand Runner When Your Boss is an Asshole…* Again, I couldn't believe it… someone noticed me? Someone knew I existed? Every day for the next week I found sweet little treasures on my desk and I couldn't help but complete my days with a grin, even in the face of corporate aggression.

On the last day I received a note that said, "I hope you enjoyed these random acts of kindness. Never give up. Pay it forward!" I could not believe that someone would be so kind as to notice me and make me feel better during a tough time. Moreover, I could not believe that somewhere in this office of mean and angry people, there was someone looking up from their desk and going out of their way to make the new girl feel happy.

That was many years ago and every time I see a new person start at the firm, I make sure their desk is full of sweet surprises during their first week. No one has ever quit within their first month and I have a sneaky feeling that random acts of kindness help them to persevere.

About the Author:
Although still in school, Belle Evelyn is the pen name of a budding writer. She manages blogs for several organizations. In addition, she likes to travel and share her life experiences.

Figure 16. How I see the world now

Pink & Polka Dotted
By Paula Wise Baker, Utah, USA

In the high desert mountains of Idaho, winter dominates the seasons. The air is uncomfortably crisp, almost sharp as it enters your lungs. As a kid, it was never a good sign when your breath began to linger in the air while waiting at the bus stop. My brothers and I were tough, though, and usually well prepared for the cold. We had to be, as Boise State football fans in the dead of winter!

When I was about nine or ten years old, the cold came really early and I did not yet have a coat that fit. My mom and dad, as a janitor and a construction worker, did not have the money to get me one until the next payday. It wasn't that bad because my mom was driving us to and from school at the time. Recess was the only real problem, because I couldn't always stay inside.

As a precocious child, I knew that my mom was upset about the state of my outerwear. My mom and dad did everything in their power to give us what we needed, but money was always tight. A new coat wasn't in the budget just yet and my parents must have been out of things to pawn at the time. It was probably really hard to see their beloved daughter without something she needed; but my parents always found a way in the end. My mom later told me that her faith as a Christian always got her through those hard times. I guess in her heart she knew that her God would provide for us.

I never was as sure as she about God and worried about how hard my parents worked. They were tired and stressed and I wanted more for them, even at such a young age. I didn't want them to worry anymore, especially not about me.

One day after an outside recess, a school nurse noticed that I didn't have a coat and remembered one my size in the lost and found. She took it home and washed it with me in mind. My teacher gave it to me one day to wear as a "loaner." It was pink with black polka dots and it fit me perfectly. I really fell in love with the way it looked and felt so happy that someone had thought of me!

I also noticed the way my mom looked when she saw me wearing a warm coat and a radiant smile. By giving me a coat, the school nurse took some of the worry away, providing my mother with relief and me with comfort.

My elementary school nurse showed me the power of giving that day. I saw in my mother's glassy and exhausted eyes that she was relieved and grateful I had a coat. I could tell that the nurse helped my mom feel better. I could also see how happy the nurse was to help our family out in a pinch. I saw that everyone truly benefitted in their own ways.

With a compassionate eye a woman saw that I was cold and she saw a way to fix it. Cynics might say "well, it wasn't really any cost to her" and dismiss the act completely. With my experiences as a young adult in mind, I think it is remarkable that she saw a problem and simultaneously began looking for a solution. It is even more remarkable that she followed through and took the extra time to ensure I would be comfortable in a clean coat.

With 20/20 hindsight, I now know that moments like this are too rare to dismiss. It is so easy for adults to get wrapped up in, well … being adults. Being thoughtful and considerate isn't always high on the priority list of the overtaxed middle class. With the average American workweek now equaling fifty-five hours, I am not at all surprised either. It is hard to provide for the emotional needs of others, when your own emotional tank is empty or maybe even broken.

Still, I frequently tell the story of my pink coat to people who ask about my motivation for giving. Along with many examples from my parents, I keep this memory as inspiration to help those in need whenever I can. It still amazes me to this day the impact such a small, random act of kindness can make.

It urges me to resist the natural feeling to just ignore another person's discomfort because I may not receive the same kindness myself. It urges me to address an issue and do my best to offer succor.

Giving – whether it is a random act of kindness or an elaborate plan for a friend – has the power to change the world. It is an amazing thing to be able to change the life of another person just by being a positive and considerate human being. This kind of giving costs so little, but the return on investment is astronomical and long-lasting. Giving will be the foundation of the rising global community and in my opinion, the foundation for a more harmonious existence.

About the Author:

Paula Wise Baker is a medical laboratory scientist and writer with big dreams. Originally from Boise, Idaho, she currently lives in Salt Lake City, Utah, with her husband and "fur babies". She has a passion for learning and empowering others to achieve their goals. Though most of her interests are scientific, she loves humans and all the strange things they do and say! As a lifelong people watcher, she has tried to pay forward the kindness shown to her by really listening to the patients she encounters and genuinely trying to connect with those that need it.

Sent from Heaven
By Netra Manjunath, India

On that bright sunny day, I could hear the birds greet me as soon as I woke up. Being a Sunday, I wanted to sleep a tad more but that would not be acceptable – if I didn't want to be the worst uncle known to mankind. It was an important day for all of us! The birds reminded me to get up. My older sister, who was very pregnant, was ready to deliver at any minute. We had been waiting for her, a long time...

Being very young, I was eager to hold a small baby in my arms. A few years ago, my sister had given birth to a lovely baby boy. But he was only five years younger than me, so it wouldn't have been suitable for me to hold him then. Now, I was starting to get stubble on my face. This was my first chance to practice being a dad! I was pretty excited.

From the other room, I could hear my sister pushing. In the 1980s, the walls were thin. We didn't have many extravagances... We couldn't really afford a flashy hospital. Back then, government hospitals in India weren't really clean. There was the worry of contracting diseases there. During my sister's first pregnancy, we'd had a bad experience with a midwife. So, we didn't want to take that route either. So, we kept her at home for as long as we could.

Walking into her room, I noticed she was moaning and shifting restlessly. Beads of sweat soaked her damp hair and glued it to her face. Though in pain, my sister seemed calm. As a nurse, she seemed to naturally understand the process and could wait and endure... After a moment or two, she looked at me. The sadness in her eyes was understood; it didn't come from physical hurt.

I'm sure she missed her husband and could have used his presence... Determined as I was to be a father figure, even I knew, I was a poor substitute. Unfortunately, her husband wasn't really interested in her pregnancy. I guess he found it difficult to provide for his family when he was just a laborer in a construction firm. A daily wage made it hard to leave when you had mouths to feed.

"How do you feel?" I asked in my most nurturing voice.

"Have been better," she replied softly and closed her eyes.

I touched her stomach and smiled as the baby kicked. I guessed he/she wanted to get out soon, too, and explore the world.

After a few hours, it was time; we brought her to the hospital. I trudged along anxiously, praying that everything would turn out alright. She was carried into a general ward.

From a distance, I saw numerous other pregnant women who'd been admitted there.

There was a monotonous mixture of loud, groaning voices in pain. All of us waited, but we didn't see a doctor tending to my sister. Of course, it might be hard for one to tend to all in a hospital with over 400 patients, hard for him to come right away... After what seemed like an eternity, the nurse finally announced that we had a baby boy. Excited, I went in to meet her. I smiled at my sister and noticed her weary expression. She had tears in her eyes but I wasn't sure if they were tears of joy or tears of pain due to numerous hours of intense pain.

Exhilarated, I lifted the baby in my arms. I'm sure I'd never felt so happy before. He was the most beautiful creature, despite being squishy and reddish. Peeling my eyes away, I noticed that all the pregnant women, including the ones who had just delivered, were lined up in beds in the ward side by side. I turned and looked at my exhausted sister's face, expecting to see her smiling at a job well done, but instead she was staring at something else intently. Twisting my body to follow her line of vision, I saw a lonely baby crying in a small makeshift crib...

There were no separate wards. The baby was right in the next bed; we could see him clearly. He looked exhausted from crying... His sobs were half choked out. It was the saddest thing... My heart felt pain. Still weak from labor, my sister nonetheless called a nurse. To her surprise, she inquired about the baby's mother. The nurse searched for the mother but we later realized that the mother had just abandoned the baby. In India, a country with an overwhelming population, we had heard of so many cases like these... Many women abandon their babies, often times, because of poverty and fear.

Sighing, the nurse told us that it was difficult to keep an eye on patients as the hospital was so overcrowded. The facilities were next to nil; it was hard to handle so many things at once. My sister nodded in understanding, as she was a nurse in the same hospital. Nonetheless, I was horrified and felt a sinking sensation in my stomach. Fearing the answer, I wondered what would happen to the baby... Just as I was about to form a question, the nurse told me that he would be given to an orphanage. The little one's future seemed bleak. I felt very sorry for him.

With the nurse's permission, I asked to hold him. Devastated, I carried him in my arms trying to think of a plan. During this, my sister took a keen interest in him. He didn't appear very healthy. Softly, she told me that his chances for survival were small. I didn't know what else to do but stare at the baby and hold it and wish it would be okay.

Raising her chin with determination, she said "I'll take him home."

I gasped.

"If I don't, he won't survive... "

"We know what happens to babies like him."

"He could be sold to some gang. They might make him do things..."

Her voice trailed off.

Astonished by my sister's declaration, I wondered how she would take care of *two* babies. She barely had money to survive! Her husband, while a hard worker, wasn't thrilled with her second pregnancy. There was a chance he wouldn't accept this. Before I could say anything, she said, "I know what you're thinking, but I'll manage and if he doesn't accept me, that's fine with me, too."

Looking at the baby's wrinkly face, she added, "I really feel bad for this baby. He looks weak and I'm certain we met each other for a reason. If I don't take him home, I won't be able to live with the guilt forever." She was firm, her eyes shining brightly and fiercely.

Proud of her, I nodded, wishing I could do more-- realizing how far I had to go to be grown up.

"I'll just work extra shifts," she stated.

She was smiling on the outside, but I knew she was really worried. In fact, she was putting up a brave front. Though her husband never reciprocated with the same emotions, she still loved him. It was a huge commitment to adopt a baby, considering their financial situation. Although a noble deed, I wondered how this would work...

She would have to stretch her working hours a lot more to take care of all the babies and her children. I wondered if she would be stuck to working twenty-four hours a day. Still in school, I was too young to help other than to encourage her and help her with her resolve to save this baby. Looking at the baby's forlorn eyes, I was happy that he'd found a mother. I couldn't imagine why his birth mother had abandoned him, but unfortunately she had.

We spoke to the nurse and since she knew my sister, we didn't have to go through formal rules and regulations. With so many babies abandoned, I think she was happy that someone cared enough to do something. We left the hospital as discreetly as we could, clutching both the babies in our arms.

&

Later, unfortunately, as expected, her husband left her. My sister told the truth. She embraced the situation and the consequences of her decision. She had to do what she felt was right. She worked longer hours and was able to provide for all of them just fine. Perhaps it was her determination that made it possible. All mouths were fed.

It was wonderful to see her love the baby as if he was her own. Truly, if she hadn't rescued him, that baby could have landed in the wrong hands or in a morgue. She took care of him for years by working as much as she could. Although without a father, they were a happy family.

Eventually, the baby grew up to be a handsome, intelligent man, who adored his mother. Years down the line, two of her own children left her as times were rough, but he stuck with her. She fell ill later but he never left her side. Perhaps God really did make them meet for a reason. They both turned out to be angels, for one other, sent from heaven.

A kind deed ended up changing their lives and inspiring me. Some moments in life you have the opportunity to make a great difference for someone else. It is a pivotal opportunity. Perhaps you will suffer great hardship, but something great will always come out of goodness.

This story was written from the perspective of the author's father about her aunt and adopted son.

About the Author:

Netra Manjunath loves to write about incidents that change the way the world thinks. As an avid reader, she also loves to read books that evoke warm, fuzzy feelings. In addition, she enjoys travelling and discovering new places. If any of her stories make even one person smile and he or she helps others, she feels like it's totally worth it.

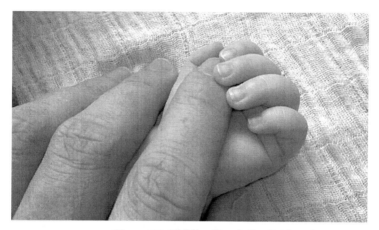

Figure 17. Holding hands for the first time

Simple Encouragement
By Samantha Loomis, Wisconsin, USA

I remember the weather perfectly. A drab day, one where pajamas and a bowl of popcorn sound like a perfect way to spend the day, curled up with a good book or a favorite movie. I waited patiently for the bus, my nylon rain jacket getting spattered faintly with rain drops. I didn't have anything to look forward to, except for the day to be over… It had been a rough week. I wasn't expecting there to be a silver lining in my rain cloud that day any time soon.

The morning came and went, filled with my usual classes and chats with friends. It wasn't until after lunch period that I heard my name called over the loudspeaker to receive a pass to come to the office. This not being a usual occurrence, me not being involved in many activities or sports (my passion for reading took up most of my time), I was astonished that there was something waiting especially for me in our school office.

My heart leapt a little, imagining what it could be. Maybe a phone call from my mother or maybe not, since she didn't seem to put much effort into our relationship anymore… actually I couldn't imagine what it could be! Depositing my things in my small hallway locker, I hurried to see what was in store.

Before I entered, I could see through the wraparound window a small bag resting on the main desk. It was a miniature white paper bag, with a red heart drawn lopsided on it. I entered and told the secretary my name; I watched her hand expectantly as she reached for the little bag. I took it from her with a nod and polite thank you, and then it was in my hands.

Not to seem too eager, I waited until I was back at my locker before tearing apart the top, staples flying. Inside was a pile of candy; I remember thinking *what in the world?* After some digging, I discovered a gift card for a local retailer hidden underneath. I dropped the bag, candy and sweets forgotten, gift card in hand. The outside of the envelope read "$10." Ten dollars? For myself?

A smile itched on my face. My mom rarely gave me spending money, and a treat like this was completely unexpected. I was excited, fantasizing about a book I could buy or maybe a new top.

It wasn't until I had tucked the gift card in my pocket and was halfway back to class (candy cached in my locker for later of course), that I realized I hadn't checked who the gift was from! My cheeks heated with shame, and I fumbled the card from its miniature envelope.

Inside the message read, "To Samantha, someone has told us you could use something special. Buy yourself a treat." I couldn't say if I stopped walking or if I made it back to class on time, but I can say what I felt.

My heart warmed with the thought that someone was thinking of me. I wasn't used to feeling special. I had woken up that day with unhappy thoughts; I was so used to working almost thirty hours a week to pay all my bills and did not have the happiest home life. However, I ended that day with a hopeful light in my eyes. I can recall that feeling today, that someone had it in their heart to randomly share their kindness with me. I thank whoever gave me a ray of sunshine during my rainy day.

About the Author:
Samantha Loomis is a junior at the University of Wisconsin-La Crosse, passionate about literature and writing. She enjoys unlimited amounts of cozy reading spaces, homemade taco dip and freshly picked strawberries. She writes for several publications and is excited about where life will take her next.

Singing for My Fare
By Christina Boyes, Pennsylvania, USA

College wasn't easy. To further myself, I moved to a new city and found a job so I could go to a decent school. Not qualifying for a full tuition scholarship, I had to pay my own way. It was a struggle to keep up with classes and work. To be cheap and save money, I took a commute over an hour and fifteen minutes away by bus because I could get the cheapest housing if I lived with three roommates in a shack a long way off from the good part of town. Sometimes, I just didn't have the fare to get from one place to another. Those days were miserable.

Lonely and exhausted, I had one tried and true source of comfort in college – music. Singing was my passion. It was what I studied. It was everything I experienced, in my clubs and activities and spare time. I was a songbird in human form. Sometimes, on the bus, I'd sing to myself to beat the blues away. Maybe they heard my lyrics. Maybe it was just the sad expression on my face. But the bus drivers noticed me.

Realizing my plight, the drivers on three of the routes I commonly rode offered me a trade. They would give me a free ride if I would sing requests for them. It was a great deal for me.

One driver gave me Eva Cassidy's "Songbird" CD as a request list. This was a Godsend. Another driver asked me for jazz standards and chided me for losing too much weight when I went on a health kick one spring. Jazz was new for me – I'd been singing swing for years, but never stepped out of the forties until he suggested it...

Over the months of commuting to and from the city, I paid when I could and sang when I couldn't. Few people can have as much impact on a self-funded college goer's life as the ones who offer the two most precious commodities: food and transportation. We became close. They took pity on me and, at the same time, gave me confidence in my voice – something I had lacked.

Pittsburgh's bus drivers fed my soul.

When nights were long, I was working around the clock to make ends meet on an income that was barely worth mentioning. Oftentimes, I didn't know where my next meal was coming from. Having people help me out when I needed it was a boon. It was more than just the ride itself. It was humans helping humans. We took care of each other. We learned about each other. We grew up together.

One of my jazz-loving drivers offered me a job recommendation for the now-defunct Dowe's on 9th. It was there that I eventually found myself. I learned to improve my voice from the extremely talented Etta Cox.

There, I met my future husband, as well as many other dear friends…

The kindness of the three bus drivers gave me more than transportation. It brought me to life and helped me to grow into adulthood a little less awkwardly. I still have the Eva Cassidy CD in my home collection, and think of Mike – the driver of the 67A route – every time I listen to it. Our paths parted after their contract negotiations shifted their routes. I ended up graduating and moving to a new location, but I haven't forgotten them in my new city.

Thanks to Mike, Mike, and Mack. Wherever you are today, memories of you are in my heart.

About the Author

Christina Boyes is a writer and digital marketing professional. She uses her knowledge and experience of life in multiple countries to provide a unique perspective on issues. She holds an M.A. in cross-cultural conflict, and hopes to complete a doctorate in Political Science in the near future. She still sings – although now most of her voice talent is directed at soothing her happy-go-lucky toddler. Christina is also the writer behind *Half Glass of Water*, a blog that examines civil wars from an interdisciplinary lens. She is also in the final stages of writing a book titled *Motherhood: From the Trenches*, which provides a humorous journey behind the scenes of motherhood, while providing practical parenting advice based on current research.

Special Delivery

By Barbara Bergerson, New York, USA

One pebble in the pond can make a beautiful pattern in the lake. Kindness has a rippling effect, too. Strangers made possible the delivery of a special message, which otherwise would not have been able to make its way to me. To this day, I smile to think of it.

One day, I stopped in the faculty office to check my mailbox as usual. I'd turned towards the counter and Paula, our mail sorter, a woman in her mid-fifties, who always had a smile on her face, showed me a curiously addressed envelope. The exterior was simply addressed to: Ms B, Wellsville, NY 14. In New York, you can imagine there are many Ms. Bs, even in the small town of Wellsville.

Anyways, Paula knew that the students quite often called me Ms. B. She went on to explain that when the mail carrier brought in the mail, he showed her the envelope and asked if it possibly could be intended for a teacher? When Paula saw the envelope, she immediately thought about me and saved it.

&

As a teacher, sometimes I wonder how much of an impact I have on my students... I enjoy teaching very much; it is my life's calling, but I always wonder if my students teach me more than I do them. I wonder if I impact them as much as they do me.

From time to time, I have the pleasure of hosting a foreign exchange student in my class. One such student, who came from abroad from Germany, was Eva. Three years ago, Eva participated in my psychology and sociology classes. During one of the classes, we were putting together a special type of puzzle. The puzzle contained 9 square pieces that had to be arranged in a specific order to complete a pattern. Right away, I could see that Eva, who was participating in a foreign exchange student program to better her English speaking skills, loved the challenge. Embracing it wholeheartedly, she quickly figured out how to master it. That's how brilliant and engaged she was.

One day Eva and another student came to my classroom during lunch, and asked if they could try some of the other puzzles. Of course, I obliged them, as Eva seemed to have such a joy in and a natural gift for puzzle-solving. Soon after that, Eva and some of her classmates joined me at lunchtime every Friday. We had fun with our little lunchtime puzzles and games.... During this time, Eva was adjusting to life in the USA. We discussed many things. Consequently, Eva certainly held a special spot in my heart.

When Eva left to go back to Germany, it was hard saying goodbye. Yet, I knew she was eager to see her family and friends and would be starting college upon her return.

From time to time, my students and I would wonder how Eva was doing.

&

With great anticipation, the office staff watched as I gingerly opened the envelope. (After all, if the letter didn't belong to me, I wanted to be able to reseal it.)

From the smile that appeared on my face, everyone knew that the contents of the envelope were indeed intended for me. It was a beautiful handwritten letter from Eva telling me how well things were going for her. She ended the letter thanking me for the positive impact I had on her life. These are the words teachers dream of hearing.

Not long after, I realized the envelope had taken quite an adventurous route to get to me.

Paula and I discussed it at great length and mused on its arrival. We did some digging and interviewing of the postal deliverer, and we examined the envelope at great length. Finally, we were able to partially trace the great adventure the letter had made to in order to get to me.

First the envelope traveled from Germany to the USA, as Eva lives there and was there at the time of the mailing. This was a feat because nowhere on the package did it say USA on the outside – nor was it labeled in German. But, someone in Germany had routed it to NY, USA!

Upon arriving in New York, it made it made its way to New York State, as opposed to the city! It did this with just a partial zip code! Handwriting, different from Eva's – probably some stranger's along the route – completed the zip code with a marker!

Next, according to the postman, the envelope arrived at the Wellsville Post Office. That would be fine except Westville has a population of 1,819. Apparently, the Postmaster polled his staff to see if they had any ideas of who "Ms B" might be! Instead of the giving up there, one of the mail carriers thought possibly a teacher might be Ms B and gave the envelope to the school, where it arrived to Paula. And, finally, to me.

So much effort was put into making this letter find its way to me! Actually, it is Wellsville, not Westville and the population is about 15,000. This precious act of kindness has stayed with me over the years. The contents were beautiful and so was the journey the letter took to get here.

Thinking back on it, whenever I find myself in a situation where I initially don't want to be bothered to do the right or caring thing, I'm reminded of all the effort that others put forth for me to receive Eva's letter. I remember how much impact that had on me and I am encouraged to do better and pay it forward.

As a result, I started doing small things to help out others. It became a habit. Then, a routine. Now, at least once a week, I intentionally do a random act of kindness… pay for someone's dinner, offer someone to go ahead of me in line, bring up the neighbor's garbage can from the curb, or offer to watch a friend's kids so they can enjoy a date night…

I found the more I focus on being kind towards others, the more I realize how just a little bit of kindness can become a huge blessing both to the recipient and to myself. More times than not, the small gesture that I make seems to be exactly what that person needs.

For example, just the simple act of letting a man go ahead of me in the checkout line at the grocery store can have a big impact. I did this one day for a stranger. He told me his wife was sick and he was grabbing milk and bread so that their kids could have breakfast before the bus came. I told him that I hoped his wife would be feeling better soon and that he was a good dad in caring for the kids. The man looked at me with tears in his eyes and said that it had been a long time since anyone told him that he was a good dad. As he left the store, I could see the bounce in his walk and I could only hope that his day continued to get better.

Random acts of kindness… they don't need to be elaborate or expensive. Rather, they just need to come from the heart. The more you shower kindness on others, the more blessings will fall upon you.

To think, it all started with receiving a simple letter.

About the Author
Barbara Bergerson resides in Wellsville, New York. She taught special education for twelve years, followed by seven years of administration. Barbara currently shares her passion for education by teaching in a jail setting. In addition to teaching, Barbara serves as a part-time church administrative assistant and enjoys writing.

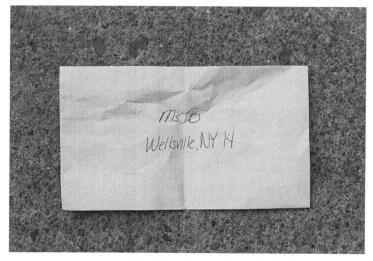

Figure 18. Would you know whom this belongs to?

Strangers in a New City
By Joanna Hoyt, New York, USA

When I made my first visit to New York City, I was thirty years old and woefully unprepared by any of my previous life experiences. I'd spent my life in small towns containing more trees than people, and I struggled with anxiety. So the Big Apple struck me as an alien planet, fascinating, incomprehensible and vaguely alarming. There was too much light, too much noise, too much happening at once for me to process. I was suffering from serious sensory overload.

I was also trying to figure out city etiquette. Where I come from it's only polite to smile and wave at people who pass you on the street. I gathered that this wasn't common practice in New York. There were people everywhere. They didn't look at each other. I slowly learned to put my hands down at my sides.

I was a fish out of water, trying to rush against the current.

By my second day in the city I felt like a three-year-old in desperate need of a nap. Nowhere was there a place to rest my ears or my eyes. Noise, movement, and lights flashed and dazzled on every street corner. The city was alive at all hours. I couldn't find enough quiet to allow me to absorb my surroundings, let alone breathe. I could barely process my thoughts, let alone navigate. People were everywhere: big, beautiful, tall, short, colorful, wild – of all shapes and sizes—but none of them looked back at me when I looked at them.

My city-bred friend Susannah's words echoed in my memory. "Don't look at people. They'll think it's rude."

When I was eleven I went for the first time to visit Susannah in Boston. I had found Boston dauntingly loud, large, and fast... But this was on a whole other level. My friend Susannah had grown up in New York City and she often said that Boston was a "friendly, little toy town." I had no idea what she meant by that. Susannah would cross crowded multi-lane streets with amazing nonchalance. I'd follow her with a mixture of trust and terror. She'd keep elbowing me to go faster and tell me to stop looking at people. Making eye contact, she'd instructed, was rude and possibly dangerous. I didn't see why it should be dangerous, but the city was her world, not mine, and I figured she must know. I reminded myself of her advice, and added a reminder to keep breathing in and breathing out.

I'd come to the city to speak at a Quaker school; a friend of the school put me up overnight. She was very kind but plainly didn't understand how foreign I felt in the city. I tried to act confident and competent, but I did admit that I had a hard time with directions. She listened and printed out a highly illustrative map to help me find my way to the school in the morning. It was printed with a nice large-sized font. We went over it a couple of times, just to make sure I would get it right. I tried to act as though the directions were as straightforward as she seemed to think they were.

Over breakfast, we decided there'd be time before I was scheduled to speak at the school to run some errands, perhaps stop by a small local Bible study. That seemed like a lovely idea! Bible study was familiar and comforting—until the end when my hostess informed me that she had to head back home, leaving me to walk two miles to the school, starting from a position that was not on my map. My hostess assured me that I'd be fine, and added that she wanted me to drop off a package for her at a church along the way. More proud than prudent, I nodded and smiled and apparently succeeded in masking my inner terror.

"It's easy to find," she said, rattling off a string of directions.

To be frank, directions have never been my strong point. When I was two, I taught myself to read. I was puzzled when my friends couldn't read the stories I wrote out carefully in my best block print. My mother was equally puzzled by the fact that I struggled to tie my shoes even at the age of six. And when I learned to drive people looked at me with the same kind of puzzlement when I couldn't remember how to get to some place that I'd gone over and over again. If I had exact directions written down, I could follow them. Otherwise, I was out of luck. I tried asking my hostess to write down her directions in as casual and nonchalant of a manner as I could muster.

"Oh, it's easy," she kept saying. "You'll be fine."

I nodded, trying to remember what she was saying, trying hard not to look clueless and worried. I must have succeeded in the latter attempt, because she went away smiling. I hadn't gone *very* many blocks before I realized that I had failed in the first attempt. I hadn't come to the cross street I was looking for. Although I hadn't meant to make any turns, according to the signs I was no longer on the street where I had started out.

Probably, it didn't help that more than half my mind was preoccupied with worry about street crossings and with the constant flow of people. I was carefully not looking at anyone for too long. This was no easy feat. My natural instinct, wanting help, was to make eye contact and hope for a sympathetic response.

My mind churned wildly.

There's a bunch of teenagers with ear buds.

...a man walking a huge white dog.

...a woman waving a pile of leaflets.

...a man hunched up and talking on his cell phone.

... a very pale-skinned woman in high heels walking fast and frowning.

...a gaggle of people with shopping bags and lots of jewelry...

... a woman who seems to be swearing at someone who isn't there...

No one seemed scary to me, but I felt overwhelmed. Certainly, I'd worked at a community center before, which had neighbors and guests of all colors and ages. Some of them struggled with mental health issues more challenging than the anxiety that had plagued me for several years. But I could meet and deal with those people one at a time. Here, there were far too many. I didn't know how to respond to them. There was no way to stop seeing them, though apparently it was safer not to look at them.

Half an hour later, I decided to stop worrying about looking at people. This was my first step towards progress, although I still hadn't figured out how to walk into any place in the vicinity of my map. Compounding the problem, the time that I was supposed to speak at the school was rapidly approaching. Unfortunately, I still didn't even know if I was going in the right direction... Frantically, I started *trying* to catch people's eyes. Nobody swore at me. Nobody looked at me, either.

Eventually, it occurred to me that passersby might think I was panhandling. Certainly, I didn't look like the city people. I mean, I was wearing what I considered presentable clothes: clean unfaded jeans and a big bright purple new-from-the-thrift-store winter jacket. Most of the people around me didn't just wear clothes; they wore *outfits* that looked as though they had been assembled to say something. I wasn't sure what my clothes said, but I was pretty sure that my facial expression said Needs Help.

Eventually, I worked up the courage to ramp up my game, as the stakes were getting higher. I tried strolling up to the edge of a group of pedestrians and saying loudly, "Excuse me, I'm trying to find..." Someone would point and I would scurry off in the direction indicated until I found another bunch of people to ask.

At last I hit one of the roads on my map at last. I was elated until I realized that I didn't know which way I needed to go on it.

Being reckless, I took a "best" guess and found myself in an area with fewer people. It was easier on my brain to have only one or two people in my field of vision at a time, but it made communication harder. The women walking alone ignored my questions and my attempts at eye contact. That unnerved me, and also made me think that maybe it was smarter for me not to try approaching any of the solitary men. I was starting to panic, and also to think that it was probably unsafe to walk down an unknown street in a strange city while visibly panicking.

Finally, there was a man alone on the corner. He was a large black man with gray in his hair and clothes that looked more like clothes than like an outfit, leaning against a railing ahead of me. He caught my eye and smiled as I approached. I smiled back at him, thinking *Don't act unfriendly* and *A woman alone in a city isn't supposed to ask help from strange men* and *He actually looked at me, maybe he'll tell me where I am.* I slowed down.

"How are you?" he asked.

"Okay, just..." There was a long pause. "I'm lost," I finally conceded. "It's my first time in the city and I'm trying to find this church and I keep getting turned around..."

He did not turn away. His friendly countenance did not change.

"You're almost there," he said. He proceeded to give me what sounded like a simple set of directions. I couldn't see the first landmark he seemed to be pointing at, but doubtless if I walked that way it would become clear, I thought... I thanked him and started off, slowing down as I got further down the road and still didn't see my marker. I turned to see my helper watching me.

He came up beside me. "You really are lost, aren't you?" he said. "Come on, I can take you there."

I stammered thanks, embarrassed by my own cluelessness, and said I didn't want to keep him if he was busy. Fortunately, he said he wasn't that busy, and it wasn't a long walk, and he'd rather just make sure I got where I was going. He talked about the weather in the tone I might have used at home to reassure a fractious goat or a frightened child. I felt myself relaxing. He brought me right to the doorstep of the church. I thanked him profusely. He looked thoughtfully at me and said, "I'm glad to help. I'd been thinking it would be nice if you had some money to give me, but I can see you're a servant too, you don't have extra money. God bless you."

I thought of saying I wasn't a servant. I was grateful for his blessing and his guidance and didn't feel like quibbling. Later, after I had delivered the box to the church and set off toward the school, helped by my map (onto which he had led me) and by my newfound confidence in the helpfulness of strangers in the city, it occurred to me that maybe his whole statement had been correct. I wasn't a servant to someone with more money, but I was trying to serve God and my neighbors, and plainly he was too. Maybe that was how he'd meant it.

I thought, too, of the people who had sometimes looked at me with apprehension as I had looked at the city people. The Latino migrant workers who my family met through a church group hesitated to sit down to a meal with us, explaining that "pure Anglos" didn't usually eat with them. The woman who came out to our farm so that exercise and time in nature could ease her anxiety and panic attacks sometimes expressed fear that we'd think her "crazy" and not want to see her again. I wished they would get over their worries and be at ease with me. I realized then, and I try to remember now, that I need to let go of my own worries, to trust and serve my neighbors.

About the Author:
Joanna Hoyt lives and volunteers full-time with her family on a Catholic Worker farm in upstate New York. During the days she tends gardens, goats, and guests; in the evenings she reads and writes eclectically. She enjoys listening to and working with people from different economic, cultural, and ideological heritages, and finding common ground.

Super Mario
By Marieta Plamenova, Bulgaria

Fourteen years ago, Mario was born in a small town in northwest Bulgaria. He was the second of four brothers but when his parents split, his mother decided that she had neither the ability nor the money to take care of the boys, and they all went to an orphanage less than a mile away from their home.

Although life was not kind to Mario, he was grateful that he could live with his brothers and they could still be a family even without their mother and father. Besides, Mario had a dream. He wanted to become a soccer star, and he used every minute away from school to play in the courtyard of the orphanage.

This was exactly where he was on November 23rd when he heard someone crying and screaming for help. Mario's native town was small but famous. It was the home of the incredible Belogradchik Rocks: a landmark of strangely shaped rock formations in red and yellow, often described as one of the most popular tourist attractions in the country. The screams were coming from the Rocks. Over the years spent at the orphanage, Mario had learnt never to leave the courtyard without permission, but there was no time for following the rules. In less than two minutes Mario reached the Rocks and saw Shaban and Nicholas, two seven-year-old boys, crying and pointing their fingers towards a 33-foot-deep trench. There on the bottom of the trench was their friend Michael, who'd fallen while playing. Without any hesitation and risking his own life, Mario climbed down to Michael who was bleeding and unconscious. Mario was not a strong boy, since the food they got was never enough at the orphanage, but he managed to put Michael on his back and climbed up with the unconscious boy. To this day, he can't explain how he got the strength to do that. He walked to the hospital still carrying Michael because, he decided, he had no time to wait for help. And he was right. The doctors took care of the unconscious boy admitting that any delay would have been fatal.

Mario was used to taking care of his brothers, and maybe that's why he didn't hesitate risking his own life to help another boy. But what he did changed his life completely. There were many people who wanted to help him after hearing the story from his aunt. Some brought food and candy to the orphanage, others sent sports equipment. Mario got a T-shirt of his favorite soccer team, Chelsea, and he didn't want to take it off even when going to bed. Then a week later the head of the orphanage got an unexpected call from the most popular soccer club in the country, offering Mario a full scholarship and a chance to join their youth team. This offer broke Mario's heart because he had to refuse it. "I can't leave my brothers," was the only thing he said, and his eyes were full with tears.

Today Mario still lives at the orphanage and plays soccer in the courtyard. Michael's parents bring firewood every winter because otherwise the children at the orphanage have to shiver in the cold. Mario's heart would never be cold, though, as long as he is with his brothers.

About the Author:

Marieta Plamenova is thirty-two years old. She grew up in a small town in Bulgaria and studied law there. Now she works as a translator and counselor in the capital, Sofia. She loves traveling and visiting new places. At home, she enjoys cooking. Her mom is a speech therapist and sometimes works with the kids from the orphanage for free and that is how she encountered Mario.

Figure 19. Belogradchik Rocks

The Deadline
By Ajit Kumar Jha, India

Three years ago I was working for a client, Margaret Kanguru, as a freelance writer. Over a period of time, we'd developed a healthy level of trust in our professional relationship, despite never having met or seen each other in person, as I am based halfway across the globe from her. Trusting me, Margaret would usually ask me first if I was available to do her work. I never refused an assignment for her, whether or not I was busy, because of how much I enjoyed working for her. The wage she offered for her jobs was fair, too.

Being proud of my work and wanting to nurture this relationship, I never failed in my commitments to her. In general, I make a point of meeting all my deadlines. But, I distinctly remember one time that I couldn't deliver the job in time...

It was an urgent assignment. This job had to be delivered within the day.

While working on this project, I got a phone call from someone who used to be my neighbor but had recently moved elsewhere. My neighbors, Tanmay and Alka Pandey informed me that their daughter, Khushi, who was about five years of age, had hurt herself terribly while playing and they knew no one in the new neighborhood. The girl had fallen on a glass table and broke the glass into several pieces! Some shards wounded her; a piece of broken glass, in fact, had scraped her neck. My neighbors were terribly worried.

Conflicted, I didn't know whether or not to rush to the hospital where they were taking the child, or to continue working on the job that was to be urgently delivered. I decided that they had called me for a reason, wanting someone to be there with them. It was already eight o'clock at night and the work had to be delivered within the next two hours. I knew if I went to the hospital to visit the little girl, I could never deliver the job in time.

Yet, I decided to rush to the hospital. The little girl was unconscious in the ICU. I stood by the parents of the little girl for several hours. The doctors informed us that she had narrowly escaped slashing her vocal cord. However, she was gradually healing.

When the parents heard this, I observed a huge sense of relief on their faces. They thanked me profusely for visiting them, while I was worried about delaying my client's work. I came back late that night. The first thing I noticed in my mailbox was a reminder from the worried client. I immediately wrote back to the client explaining the reason for the delay. I also reassured her that the job would be delivered as soon as possible. Now, I'd have to live with the consequences.

The client didn't respond to my email.

I completed the job anyway and sent it to the client early the next morning.

I received no response.

However, few days later, I received payment for the job through Western Union. The amount I received was £5 more, in addition to the agreed-upon fee for the job. The sender's note read, "The additional £5 is for your neighbor's daughter. Go buy her some candies."

About the Author:

Ajit Kumar Jha studied Philosophy at St. Stephens College, Delhi, and Sociology at Delhi School of Economics, Delhi University. Currently, he works for different clients and also writes independently on different web platforms. In the process of building his career, he claims to have learned at least two valuable lessons. First, it is not for your personal satisfaction alone that you write, rather you write for others pretty much like any other professional who works for others. Your writing is only as good as others can empathize with it. Readers empathize with your work only if it solves their problem or gives an insight into their problems. People empathize with your work only when they get a feeling of déjà or your work conforms to at least a part of their experience.

Figure 20. Khushi Pandey, my neighbor's daughter, today.

The Effects of Helping Out
By Tiffany Mcrae, Guyana

When I was fifteen, I'd often wonder if I was normal. I didn't care about the same things that most other kids did. School dances, makeup, boys and rebellion did not appeal to me so much as things older people liked, such as charity functions. I found this odd. I wanted to figure out my identity and had trouble reconciling who I was with what I was supposed to be. It stressed me out.

One day during my process of "discovering myself," I went to a local community meeting. Everyone there was older than me. However, they all seemed excited about something, which is more than I can say about most teenagers. Yeah, I was hanging out with people decades older. Who cares?

Changing our neighborhood and making it a safer place to live in appealed to me. These folks had ideas and energy. One idea they suggested was mentoring youth. A lot of school-age children end up messed up later on in life because they didn't have good role models growing up. Being swept up by the crowd, I shocked myself when I raised my hand to find out whether or not I could assist. I didn't necessarily think that I was going to be the most qualified mentor, as I was fifteen and still discovering myself, but I was certainly eager to be involved.

The next Saturday, I found myself a teacher to the young. Apparently, no one else had volunteered. This made me the de facto best candidate, as I was the only candidate. Upon learning this news, I spent the entire week preparing myself both mentally and physically. My biggest fear at the time was whether or not the children would like me. Would they think I was a fraud? How I was going to react to them? Would they want to come back after the first class? Would I get kicked out?

Finally, Saturday came. I had so much anxiety. I both wished the day would come and that it would go at the same time. Somehow though, I overrode my emotions and dragged myself down the street to the school where the kids waited for me.

Of course, in my nervousness, I missed the correct bus stop and ended up having to double back. I was late on my first day!

Approaching my destination and breathless from running, I saw a group of children sitting quietly. This reminded me of the horror movie where children waited for villagers in cornfields before they turned into demons. My first thought was they were either very well trained or had something up their sleeves. Brushing aside my paranoia, I introduced myself and gave a long apology for being late, but all they did was smile.

To my surprise, nothing awful happened in the next hour. My first class went well.

Volunteering actually made me so happy that I wanted to share my experience with my friends. One by one they joined, each giving up their Saturdays, too. There was a running joke that only a saint would give up their Saturdays for volunteering. My nickname became Mother Teresa.

Months went by quickly. The number of children in my class increased. One afternoon after class, the caretakers of the center where the class was being held said they wanted to see me. Of course, I was a bit nervous about it. I had all sorts of scenarios running through my head. Had I done something wrong? Did someone complain? Did they realize I was only fifteen?

I was pleasantly surprised when they said that they were really happy with the work I was doing with the children. The parents shared how the children in the neighborhood who were a part of the class had changed in many ways. Their words brought joy to my heart. They spoke again and said that they also wanted to assist me with transportation, as it cost me much money to travel from my part of town to theirs.

As much as I helped them, they taught me a valuable lesson. Happiness comes from within and it is all that matters. Joy comes from helping others. For all my soul-searching and trying to fit in, I really just needed to understand who I was instead of trying to mold myself into something else. I just needed to find my place, where I belonged.

About the Author:

Tiffany Mcrae works with young people in a development project based on giving service to the community. She takes residence in Guyana.

Figure 21. Community Youth Group

The Gift

By Bhavya Kaushik, India

I have never believed in angels. The idea of ordinary human beings walking among us with wings always seemed unreal to me. And not just angels – I have always found it hard to believe in anything extraordinary. But my disbelief took an unexpected turn one day, when I was hit by a walking angel.

It was almost two months back, when I was staring at a mannequin. The unanimated figure looked flawless, with its perfect curves and a strong masculine jawline. It wore dark gray trousers, which I wanted to buy. Although I knew that they wouldn't look the same on my deformed body, I still wanted to give them a try.

"Excuse me." I heard a gentle voice coming from the back, while I was looking for my size in the stack of those same trousers.

I stood up and saw a lady walking towards me. I looked at her face as she elegantly tiptoed her way – the wrinkles at beneath her emerald green eyes and the freckles on her pearl white cheeks. She looked in her early forties and had a faraway look in her eyes. Yes, she was looking at me, but her eyes were craving something, somewhere else –

beyond the horizon and definitely beyond the walls of that store.

"Yes ma'am," I replied, trying to sound as respectful as possible.

"Hi! You might find this strange. But can you do me a favor?" She asked in a very polite tone. I have never been a kind of person who helps a random stranger, but somehow that day, I couldn't say no to her beautiful face.

"Yes, what is it?"

"Actually, I have a son who looks just like you and it is his twentieth birthday today," she began to explain.

I interrupted her halfway. "Oh! I will be twenty next month, too!"

"That's great! Like I said – you both are very similar in physical appearance and age. I wanted to buy him a gift for his birthday today. But he is not with me right now. Can you help?"

With that, my eyes lit up. I have always loved shopping. The smell of fresh clothes, the thrill of selecting that one perfect outfit from a pile of hundreds, the swiping of credit cards – it all makes my world better.

So when she asked me to assist her in shopping, I replied her with a big "YES!" And we began searching for a perfect shirt.

"So what does he look like?" I asked, in order to filter some color choices.

"He looks just like you – same complexion, same height," she replied and picked up a light blue shirt from the aisle.

"Yes. This would look great!" I said in full enthusiasm, and I picked three more shirts to try.

In the next fifteen minutes, we tried every shirt that we selected, and then a couple of more. We talked about her son a lot – how he is obsessed with chocolate, just like me, his weird taste in music and unconventional sci-fi books, his dreams and his passion; and from her description, he seemed like my other half – or just a better version of me, maybe.

Finally, we selected the same light blue shirt that she'd picked earlier. Somehow the one that she picked looked perfect on me as well. It was the first time in my life that I looked as flawless at the mannequin.

"This is perfect. You should definitely buy this!" I concluded at the end, and changed back to my original attire.

"Yes, it is perfect. It brings out the sparkle in your eyes. They just somehow... lit up when you wore this," she said and hugged me tightly. That was all I wanted to hear.

"Thank you!" she finally said and let go of me.

"Do wish him a very happy birthday on my behalf as well!" I said and she replied me with a nod. I watched her walking towards the cashier and smiled. I don't know why, but there was something in her presence that made me feel content.

Later I selected the trousers that I wanted to wear for the coming formals. When I went to pay, the cashier gave me a huge smile. With that smile, he forwarded me a bag.

"The lady who was talking to you earlier told me to give this to you," he said. I kept looking at the bag with a quizzical look on my face.

"I think it's a gift," he added.

I opened the bag and found the same light blue shirt inside of it. I was ecstatic and overwhelmed. It felt like I was on cloud nine!

With that shirt, I also found a note in the bag. I couldn't stop myself from reading it right away. So, I thanked the cashier and ran to my car to read it in some peace.

Dear Stranger,

I don't know your name. But what is the significance of all these names, when one day we will all be a pack of anonymous bones.

Today when I saw you staring at a mannequin, I saw a reflection on my own son in your eyes. He died when he was six and yes, today would have been his birthday. He would be just like you. It would be his twentieth birthday today and although I could not buy him a birthday present, I wanted to.

So I bought this small gift for you. I know this will make him happy because it made me happy, too. You are such an amazing and thoughtful kid. You are everything that I wanted him to be. Funny, smart, talkative, passionate and thoughtful. I hope you will find whatever it is you are trying to find in your life. Not everyone does!

Love,

Me.

I read the letter once and I cried. I read it again after three days, when I wore the same shirt for the formals, and I cried a little more.

I still wear that shirt. I cherish it with my life. Every time I wear it, I think of her and smile. Whenever I touch the fabric of that shirt, a part of her exists inside of me – the same way that her son lives inside of her, even in his absence.

I have never believed in anything pious or extraordinary. But from that day on, I started believing in a higher power, the existence of angels and miracles. When I touched her, I realized that miracles happen and angels exist. They walk right among us. They don't have huge wings or halos; instead they have that infinite look in their eyes. I can proudly say that I'm one of those fortunate souls who witnessed a random gesture of kindness, a miracle. I was touched by an angel.

About the Author:

With a Masters in Computer Science, Bhavya Kaushik believes versatility is the key. The author of a bestselling novel, he is in pursuit of his unwavering passion to talk about things that touch our souls and leave everlasting impressions.

Figure 22. The shirt today

Rediscovering the Good Deed Game
By Leonard Treman, Michigan, USA

Relevant Pre-Story Information:

In December 2010, I tried to kill myself. When I saw the harm it was causing my family, I decided never to attempt it again out of love and respect for them. On that day, I also I decided that I would live my life for others and become a utilitarian by rule. From then on, I tried to view life less intensely, as a game, with good deeds as the score. To give my life meaning, I made an oath to attempt to get the highest score. This has become my purpose for existence.

From that point forward, anytime I've had a chance to affect the greater good, I've felt compelled to do so. When I fail to act, I consider it a sin and violation against my oath to do everything in my power to improve the world. Because of this oath, I often end up in odd situations, which nonetheless somehow turn out great. The sequence of events you are about to discover occurred in early January 2014.

With an hour left before my interview, I decided to go jogging in Birmingham, a city where the buildings are the color of money. Every third business is an investment center. The place is ripe with cash, wealth, opulence, and the nouveau riche. For my run, I started on a path and intended to do laps through this beautiful town. As I rounded around the first corner, an elderly woman dressed in fine furs slowly made her way down the middle of the sidewalk. Trying not to stop, I dashed into the road to avoid a near collision.

As I continued to the next corner on that half-mile block, I saw a police officer talking to a vagrant. Another officer poked his head out of a car window. As I got closer, I hugged the buildings, trying to avoid the crowds on the street. Still keeping my jogging pace, I mildly wondered to myself what the homeless guy had done wrong to warrant two cops questioning him.

As I rounded the bend to the next part of the block, I saw another homeless man. *I never knew there were so many of them in this area of town.* As I rounded the third bend, I saw a lingerie shop. Visions filled my head. My old girlfriend and I had walked past here, in this very spot, and I could remember being happy as we laughed and walked around. I was confident, in charge, a leader. Suddenly, surging with energy, I galloped forward in a fast sprint to outrun the memory.

I'd finished the first lap and was part of the way into the next one when I saw the police officer again. This interrupted my mindless mind chatter. Shaking myself awake, I thought about approaching him to see what it takes to become an officer. The job market is tough, and a police officer is an honorable career. As I gazed over, I noticed he was still talking to the same homeless guy. The homeless guy wasn't being arrested; he was just talking to the police officer. I was more than a bit curious as to what had been going on, but I was still trying to keep up my jog.

As I powered through toward the lingerie store again, I thought about my first kiss with that girl. Her heart was beating normally and when I pulled her in, like the patter of a rainstorm, it began to flutter against my own chest. She was gone now and I was feeling empty. I needed something to fill the void. Our combined identity as a couple had been shattered and I was having trouble adapting to becoming myself again.

As I turned the corner the third time, I was close enough to actually hear bits of the conversation. I heard the officer say, "I'm just worried about your safety. It's really cold out here," and then I passed him. Trying not to linger, I thought about how cold it was and how cold my legs were. I was wearing pants, sweatpants, socks, a shirt, a sweater, a coat, and shoes. That homeless guy was wearing about the same, but he'd been out there a lot longer. Suddenly, I felt kind of guilty for judging him.

As I rounded past the lingerie shop, I thought of why the breakup had occurred. There was a lack of communication. My girlfriend had said, "I love you, see you tomorrow." Then she kissed me goodbye.

The next day, she sent me a text saying that we were breaking up. She would not respond to a single text, phone call, or even acknowledge me when I drove to her house on the day of the breakup. I hated the lack of communication. My mind was doing curious leaps. I tried harder to shake it off.

As I rounded the bend, the officer was gone and only the homeless guy remained. He was leaning against the building and standing there peacefully. Quickly, I looked away before he could see me staring, but my curiosity remained. As I continued my pace, the second homeless guy reappeared back around the clothing shop.

As I rounded the bend again, I saw him but I couldn't bring myself to speak. He mumbled something, but I couldn't hear what. As I continued on my way, I became mad at myself. I was supposed to have helped him but I didn't do a thing. As I was contemplating my stupidity, the second homeless guy approached me. He humbly asked, "Do you have any money I could have? I am trying to get to Grace Centers of Hope in Pontiac to get some free clothing."

Seeing a chance to redeem myself, I replied. "I don't carry money on me, but I can check my car for clothing." The man began to follow me, and I turned around and said, "I'll be back in ten minutes with some clothing for you, just wait here."

The man replied, "Thanks man, I really appreciate it, I'll be waiting."

I ran to my car in the parking structure nearby. I forgot I had cleaned out my car and it was devoid of the spare clothing that I'd normally leave in there. There was only one spare shirt in my car and it was the shirt that I had last worn when my first dog Becky died, a shirt that's a personal treasure of mine. I thought to myself, *I promised and it's cold. I'll have to buy him something to keep him warm.*

Looking around me, all of the shops were ultra-expensive. Being a broke college student looking for a job at this point in my life, this was not the ideal economic environment to be purchasing coats. Suddenly, I recalled a new shop that had opened up recently. Perhaps the prices might be a little lower because of that.

I remembered it because of the giant omega symbol over the door. The shop had sweaters and exercise gear that looked warm.

As I rounded the bend, the leader in me kicked in. I walked into the shop and barked, "Hi, what's the least expensive thick sweatshirt you have?"

The man at the counter replied, "What color do you want?"

"Whatever color is the least expensive," I replied.

The man had a strange look on his face and asked, "What's this for?"

I said, "There's a homeless guy out there who needs something to keep him warm."

The man looked at me, then said, "That's really kind-hearted of you."

These words seemed foreign to me, because as I've described above, helping people was just a game to me and in the benefit of my own goals to help these people.

He thought for a second and said, "Why don't you pick out any of these sweatshirts and give it to him?"

I answered a little sheepishly, "I have to stick to the cheaper ones, I'm pretty broke right now."

"It's on the house. Due to budgeting restrictions, we can only give out one, but pick any one you think he'd like," the man said.

I was shocked at what a nice person he was, but at the same time I was happy. We were totally making this happen for that homeless man.

"Let me go get him and he can pick it out," I said.

The man smiled and said, "OK."

I dashed out toward the lingerie store to get the man and all of a sudden I heard a call, "Hey, Sir." I turned around to see the first homeless guy who the police officer was talking to earlier. He asked, "Sir, is there any way you could get me some food?"

My mind was still going, *coat, coat, coat, coat...*

"Sure," I said.

I turned around and there was a Starbucks behind me.

"What do you want from Starbucks?" I asked.

"A hot chocolate," he replied.

"Done," I responded and I walked into the Starbucks.

I smiled, I hadn't been that happy since before the breakup.

I triumphantly marched out of the coffee shop and handed the homeless guy the hot chocolate and he looked me straight in the eyes, "God bless you, you don't know how many people I have asked."

"No problem, have a safe night, dude," I replied and I headed off to get the guy who wanted the coat. The homeless guy called out, "You, too," as I was walking away.

I was swelling with pride, I felt like a cape- and costume-clad superhero flying around and saving the homeless. I'd rediscovered the key to happiness: it is helping people. I was back to my old ways again. I could start to feel my old self again.

I figuratively flew over to where the second homeless man had been and he wasn't there. I ran back and forth on the street looking for him. Poof, he was just gone. I spent the next few minutes looking for him, but he seemed to have just vanished.

I walked back to the first shop feeling like a failure. I was worried, *What if that guy freezes and it was all because I took too long.* If I found that that had happened, it would count against my "good deed score."

When I got back to the clothing shop, I walked in kind of sad. The salesclerk asked, "Where's the guy?"

"I couldn't find him," I replied, deflated.

There was a moment of silence and he said, "That was still nice of you to do."

I looked up and thought about it for a moment. I really hadn't done it to be nice, I did it for myself. Then I thought about the homeless guy who I gave a hot chocolate to. It dawned upon me, whatever my reasons were, I did do a good thing. I could feel my smile grow.

"Says the guy who was going to give away a hundred-dollar sweatshirt on a whim. You are a nice guy too. I'm going to tell everyone what you were offering to do," I said, trying to make him feel just as good about himself as he had just done for me. About two seconds later his friend came in and started to do some ridiculous dance at the entryway, and I slipped out unnoticed.

As I ran the next few laps I thought about a few things. I wanted to do this again; it made me feel happy. Surprisingly enough, when I helped that homeless man, he had also helped me. I think about the homeless man who wanted the coat a lot. My imagination runs wild.

Sometimes I imagine he was an angel here to set me on the right path. My mom thinks that he was a panhandler looking for a quick buck. Regardless of what he was, he helped me a lot. Things in my life have settled down again and I seem to have found my purpose again.

As time ticked on following the incident, things began to normalize, and I encountered my ex-girlfriend. When I looked at her, I didn't feel pain and I didn't long to be with her again. I was happy to be in my own skin. My identity was mine again, thanks, at least in part, to the events a couple of weeks earlier. While time did help, rediscovering my mission was key to recovering me.

About the Author:
Leonard Treman is a twenty-four-year-old author who writes fiction, gaming guides, and occasionally, non-fiction memoirs. He's one of those lost college grads looking for a job at the moment, but that doesn't stop him from having crazy adventures. If you are interested in some of his other works visit http://authorleonardtreman.webs.com/.

Figure 23. The street corner where this all occurred.

The Happy Meal
By Ayamma Mohsin, Pakistan

I curse under my breath, slamming the breaks as the signal turns red. The scorching heat of the midday sun feels like it's seeping through my skin, into my brain, sucking out every ounce of energy I have left in me – if any. The poor air conditioner seems like it has surrendered to the wrath of the summer sun. I look to my left at my four-year-old niece, Arya, as she wipes off a drop of sweat tickling down her forehead and resumes hunting for fries in her Happy Meal box. The endless traffic reflected in my rearview mirror adds to my agitation. *Another twenty minutes!* I think to myself, irritably.

A knock on my window – almost inaudible amid all the honking – catches my attention. Groaning in frustration, I turn to address this new nuisance. It's a child of around six or seven, a little boy. He seems small – insignificant really, in the midst of the roiling, honking sea of vehicles. Gosh, beggars! I shoo him away impatiently, my thoughts already returning to calculating how much longer till the signal turns green. He, however, continues to knock, as I chose to ignore him. *A few more seconds!* I slam my palm across the steering wheel.

The repeated knocking on my window is starting to get to me. "Go knock at some other window. I've got nothing for you!" I scream at the boy, unwinding the window. This sudden outburst startles the kid, and maybe even scares him a little, as he backs away, looking slightly hurt, and almost teary-eyed. I sigh in the momentary relief, and turn my thoughts away from that hurt face and those ragged clothes, before the guilt of it can creep up on me.

This short outburst of rage, however, has caught Arya's attention. I feel a small tug at my sleeve and turn to find her blue eyes fixated on the boy, her confusion evident.

"Why is he not wearing shoes?" she finally speaks, after a few long moments. "Why are his clothes so dirty? Why does he keep looking at me? Do you think he wants my toy? Do you think he wants my fries? Is he hungry?" She breaks into a series of unexpected questions, one after the other while I try to comprehend the words coming out of this four-year-old's mouth. She tugs at my sleeve again, whispering now. "I think he's hungry. Can I ask him if he's hungry?" At my silent approval, she shyly motions to the boy to come forward.

He looks at her, evidently confused. He points himself, questioningly, as if to ascertain she's gesturing at him. Arya nods, her small head bobbing up and down. He shoots me a cautious glance as he approaches Arya's side of the car. She unwinds her window, downright gleefully, as he finally approaches, still a little hesitant.

"Hi, my name's Arya. What's yours?" she says, reaching out to offer the boy her hand. He shakes her hand with a shy smile, finally warming up to her. "I'm Bae," he responds.

Arya looks down at the hand she holds, so frail and bony, with a slight frown on her face, as if she doesn't understand what she sees. "You sleeve is torn." she says noticing the sorry state of the Bae's shirt. "You should get your mommy to fix it. Mummy fixes the holes in my dresses all the time," Arya says with a smile on her face as she recalls how mummy patched up her skirt when she fell from the swing a few days ago.

Bae looks down, keeping his eyes firmly on the ground, and shrugs. "I don't have a mo-…" he starts to say but one look at Arya's smiling face, the innocence there, and he finishes with, "the thread…we ran out." Arya tilts her head to the side, as if in thought, and reaches over to grab her Happy Meal box. She lowers the window further down and pushes the box into Bae's unsuspecting hands.

"I can't give you any thread but you can have my fries. If you share them with your mom and ask nicely, I'm sure she'll buy some thread for you. My sister Emmy always says to share, so share it, okay?"

I watch as my niece, my *four-year-old* niece, happily gives away her favorite food in the world, as if it means nothing to her. The purity of this short exchange right in front of my eyes surprises me. How can this four-year-old girl, who knows nothing of this world beyond her fries and her toys, find in her heart to hand over something so dear to her out of the kindness of her heart, while we, being blessed enough to be sitting in our air conditioned cars, leading our luxurious lifestyles, and knowing of this world and how harsh it can get for the less fortunate, fail to extend a little help, irrespective of how insignificant to our own lives that form of help may be.

I'm startled out of my trance by a car horn, and as I hear Arya ask the boy if he has a sister, and the boy reply with a soft no, I start up the car once more. Arya seems to notice this, for she quickly pushes her stuffed elephant into his hand and shouts, "Take Elly, she can keep the bad dreams away just like Emmy does for me," her voice getting lost among the car horns and the revving sounds of engines as drivers all around start to get impatient. I start to drive away but not before seeing Arya wave enthusiastically at her new friend. I glance in the rear view mirror and see the most brilliant and sincere smile on the boy's face as he waves back and dodges cars left and right to get out of the road.

I spend the rest of the drive dazed, not because my niece is sitting next to me, humming the Dora the Explorer theme song and kicking her legs back and forth, as if parting with Elly wasn't a big deal, and not because I picked up on the sheer joy on Bae's face when Arya gave him all her riches with a smile on her face, but because I recognize the scene for what it was – an act of kindness, and more than that, an act of pure selflessness. I am proud of my niece and ashamed at my own conduct. I had shouted at him and she talked softly, I told him off and she made him her new friend, I refused to help a lost soul and she gave everything she had – God bless her kind little heart – so that he would not be so alone anymore. Arya did what I could not, nay, would not do. She helped because she could. I learnt that day that my niece, in her four years of life, had learnt how to be a generous spirit, when I, in my eighteen years, had not.

About the Author:
Ayamma is an eighteen-year-old with a passion for writing, currently pursuing her undergraduate degree at Lahore University of Management Sciences, who might just be majoring in co-curriculars rather than an actual subject, courtesy of her fondness for event management and anything that involves colors and ideas and creativity and maybe shopping. She is a hopeless optimist who thinks if

colors had characteristics (which they should), yellow would be happy. She is a sucker for rain, and sunsets, and fogs, and Nutella, and believes anything and everything can be beautiful, from an overly cheesy pizza, to a gorgeous set of antique earrings, to a four a.m. visit to the park. She loves to travel, explore places, try out food, shop, play basketball, gawk at photographs, but at the end of the day, writing is her happy place. She has a blog (more of a failed venture, at times): ayammamohsin.wordpress.com.

I don't know who, in what part of the world might be reading this, but whoever you are, and if you're in a fix, go eat a jar of Nutella, or stare at the sky, or look at a child's laugh; spread a little love – it'll make you feel better. And eventually, this time will pass. And it'll all be just fine. Lots of love!

The Seven-Fifty to Marble Arch
By Jan Gamm, Spain

Amelia met him in the fifties. He was studying law; she was a legal clerk working in a dusty office in central London, jammed between an antique book shop and an ancient church.

Her life was over-disciplined and steeped in tedium. Every evening she returned by train to her mother's grand house in Croydon, full of pre-war furniture and still carrying the scars of the Blitz, over-large for its two occupants.

Olivia had expertly kept her daughter in line since the disappearance of Amelia's father twenty years before. There were no weekly dances, no gentleman callers, in fact, there were no callers at all... Amelia was twenty-three, tall and slim, with passable features, immaculately dressed and scrupulously polite. She had never had a boyfriend and never been allowed to venture out of Croydon.

"Hello," he said, "Hold this, please," handing her a wet umbrella that dripped all over her pink bouclé suit. He was extremely tall, with rain-spattered glasses, far too thin for the gray business suit that hung loosely over his bony frame. His wet hair stuck to his forehead and a limp newspaper drooped from under his arm, smelling of soggy print. As he heaved a battered old buckle-fronted briefcase onto the overhead rack, he trod on her toe and she yelped, attracting the attention of the other travelers in the crowded carriage.

"Whoops – so sorry – always been a bit of an oaf, are you alright?" His clumsy apology was followed by a beaming smile that split his angular features in two and lit up the gloomy day.

She felt the redness creeping up from her neck and stammered quickly, "Yes, I'm fine, don't worry about it," before anyone else could notice the embarrassing pink tide spreading over her face.

He elbowed the passengers on either side of his seat as he struggled to separate the pages of *The Times* before gallantly handing her a wet page on interior décor. The print immediately stained her white gloves but she quickly slipped them off before he noticed and brought them further attention with more stumbling apologies…

As the train jolted to a halt and the carriage quickly emptied, she made a great fuss of gathering her handbag and her own umbrella, needing to hurry to make it to her lonely office by eight-thirty but wanting to spend a few more minutes in his company. She hesitated before picking up her raincoat.

"I'm Peter," he said, picking it up for her and making no attempt to hand it over.

They got off the train together and despite her mother's vicious objections stayed together for the next fifty-five years.

Tuscany

I met her at a craft club held in a sleepy hotel in Florence, a crusty, more than slightly bossy organizer of other people's skills. She was frail at eighty-one, unable to walk steadily without the aid of a cane. Someone said she had lost her health and strength nursing her sick husband for years. She was the personality of the group, scolding latecomers and offering unwelcome opinions on the state of some of the "crafts" being made.

"Whatever is that?" she asked, pointing at a woolen blob with her cane.

"It's a donkey," said a gray-haired lady, as the owner of the blob tried unsuccessfully to hide it behind a pile of patterns.

"Well, it looks ready for the abattoir," said Amelia. "Put it on the recycling pile." She addressed me with, "Who are you? Have you brought something to do?"

"Actually I am here to write about the craft group," I started.

"Well, sit over there and try not to get in the way."

I surprised myself by staying until the end. Her masterful organizational skills fascinated me. The other members of the group smiled at her forthright criticism and not one of them took offence at her bluntness. It was obvious that they liked her.

"I suppose you would like a cup of tea," she said when we were finally left alone, the last two, reluctant to venture onto the scorching street outside.

"Yes, please," I said bravely.

She poured a strong blend of almost black tea into a delicate china cup and began to interrogate me about my life. My family, my career, my views on a dozen different topics… After twenty minutes, she promptly cut the conversation short and headed for the door.

"I have to go now. Call me," she said.

She had left her address and telephone number on a card on the table…

A Curious Friendship

Four days later, I called on her in her little bungalow in the hills. As I walked through the door I walked back in time. The walls were lined with thousands of books, tapes, records, and travel souvenirs. My mouth dropped open as I spied collections of Japanese netsuke; Chinese porcelain and jade; first editions; rare Venetian glassware… the treasure trove of art seemed to be holding up the ceilings in most of the rooms. Every square inch of Amelia's home was crammed with beautiful items, shipped from England years before when she and her husband retired to the Mediterranean...

I turned and caught her looking at me, enjoying my astonishment. Incredulous, I asked, "Are all of these yours?"

"Actually none of them," she answered. "They were all Peter's. He was something of a collector. And now I am something of a custodian, in reality a sort of prisoner of his enthusiasm for wonderful things. I could not possibly sell any of it and cannot bring myself to give any of it away because it was his treasure." She smiled sadly. "I would probably be more comfortable in a nice modern apartment in town, near to the clinic and the shops. But I cannot bear the thought of not being able to touch his books and his music. They bring him near to me."

I visited her every week after that. I learned that Peter had died three years before but before he died his illness had made him completely dependent on her for at least six years. She had fed him; bathed him; carried him to his chair; his bath; his bed... Her muscles and bones had almost been destroyed by her burden yet she spoke of him with glowing devotion.

Four years later, we have never missed our Wednesday afternoon ritual that begins shortly after lunch and ends with my rushing out of the door at nearly seven, habitually late for supper, having spent many hours of in-depth and sometimes heated discussion on current affairs, art, music, and travel.

She told me once how grateful she was for my visits. I felt guilty receiving her thanks when in fact her friendship gave me far more than she could ever imagine. Ever the practical organizer, she asked me once to write her eulogy. I cautiously agreed; half expecting her to ask me help her choose the exact wood finish on her coffin...!

"Would you please write about Peter?" she asked, "Make everyone understand how much I loved him. He saved me, you know, that day on the seven-fifty to Marble Arch. My mother was too strong for me and I would have spent my life in that house in Croydon had it not been for his love and kindness. And later, he saved me from loneliness again by sending you to me.

"I have been an administrator, legal secretary and teacher, mother of two beautiful children and grandmother of five. But most of all and forever, I was Peter's wife."

About the Author:

A prolific writer, journalist and illustrator, Jan Gamm was born in Wales but spent her childhood and teens in the Far East. She has lived and worked all over the world and now resides with her partner, close to the Mediterranean where she continues with her writing and drawing. Her books and illustrated stories have brought reading pleasure to thousands.

The Unexpected Surprise
By Paula R., Mexico

A sudden hit brought me back to this dimension; my face smashed against the window, and immediately a huge red bump started showing on my forehead.

After a few seconds, I realized someone had crashed the back of my car. I turned around, and a tiny man driving a white Chevy recklessly moved in between the traffic lines and disappeared before my eyes. This didn't surprise me, why would he care if I'm all right? Why would a stranger care if I hadn't paid my insurance and had no money to fix my car?

I arrived late for work. My boss was furious, so I had to work the whole day without getting paid. He saw the huge lump on my forehead; he saw my car was practically destroyed, but I was late, and that's all that mattered to him. Why should he care?

Of course, after work was over, I couldn't start my car so I had to take the bus home... I usually leave the office in the peak hours of the afternoon and the bus was completely jammed. There were no seats available and I had to stand near a window the whole way home. There was an old lady beside me who looked exhausted and was falling asleep even though she was standing. More than half of the people sitting on the bus were men, and not one offered to cede a seat to this lady...

In the bus everybody seemed angry about something; dark expressions, zero smiles, concealment. They were all immersed in their own thoughts, not caring or paying attention to anything around us. The world is full of evil and tiny men going crazy on the streets and uncompassionate bosses. No wonder no one laughs anymore...

When I was a block away from home, a boy ran from the back of the bus and snatched the old lady's purse from under her arm. In a quick jump, he stepped down and vanished into the dark streets. There was a moment of unsettlement inside the bus, but no one said anything about it. Soon after, everyone seemed to have forgotten about what happened, the dark aura intensified, and everybody submerged into their own problems, again.

Finally home, the bump on my forehead getting worse, I jumped into the shower and then lay down for a while to rest. I felt as if all the energy in my body had abandoned me, I couldn't do anything, so I just stared at the ceiling. Suddenly I felt my nose itching from the inside, something in my chest was bothering, my sight was clouded and something that hadn't happened in a long time occurred: I cried.

It was as if all that I had kept inside emerged uncontrollably, and a disconsolate emotion took control of my body. I cried because my head hurt, I cried because my car was ruined, I cried for the old lady. I cried because I was disappointed with people, with the world, with everything. I cried because life is not what I thought it was, because the world is not a safe place, because everyone seemed to have forgotten about love, about happiness, about generosity, about something called compassion.

I cried because I felt tired of living in a cruel world; full of injustices, of hate, of indifference. I felt tired of having been fooled, hurt and laughed at. I cried because everything I thought life was, when I was a kid, is not real; my dream of changing the world, of making it a better place seemed impossible. I cried because there are no more good people left on this world. I cried because people know they are harming people and provoking pain and they just don't care. I cried because life is not fair, because this is not how the world is supposed to be. I cried because I felt alone, because I had lost my faith in everyone and everything, I cried because I was in desperate need for something to comfort me, I was desperate for a sign, for something that could make me believe not everything is lost.

When I was almost exhausted but still restless, I turned the T.V. to help me get some sleep; I just wanted this day to be over. As I was changing channels, something unusual happened... A young man, maybe in his late twenties, was being interviewed; he was wearing a torn red sweater and had an envelope with a hundred dollars in his hand. He was crying in front of the camera, but his eyes were full of joy and gratitude.

It was a surprise to see someone crying from joy, so I kept watching, enthralled. The story was about a stranger who had used a Twitter account to randomly help people around the world. This mystery philanthropist had hidden envelopes with money all around a park that's close to my house, just to make people smile.

I lay there half asleep and half-awake, dreaming and musing on my day and this... Suddenly, I began to feel a lightness well up inside of me. A laugh broke through my dried eyes.

I'm sure the stranger has achieved his goal; I sincerely believe the man with the hundred dollars is still smiling, I absolutely believe this stranger changed something in him, and I know, this stranger changed something in me, too.

A simple act, a word, a good deed makes a difference. Sometimes it's hard to believe in generosity, perhaps because we only focus on everything that's wrong around us, things that affect us or affect the people we love, and we think there's no good on earth anymore. We are surrounded with negativity only if we focus on it; there are so many good and amazing things in life and in people, we just have to pay attention to it.

After having a really bad day, a stranger surprised me. The world is full of fantastic people that with only one gesture can make someone's life easier, better and happier, and give reasons to the rest of us to believe in human kindness.   I slept easier that night.

About the Author:
Paula R. works as a senior translator/interpreter at Televisa Networks. She is passionate about words and literature and enjoys writing in her free time. She currently lives in Mexico City.

Figure 24. My car after it got rear ended.

There's a God in Each One of Us
By Shruti Fatehpuria, India

Back in India, people say there are more festivals than a person can count. There are more Gods than you can memorize and almost every other place is a pilgrimage. I come from a God-loving family and thus it was no surprise that we had various trips that focused more on travelling to temples than enjoying the beaches.

However, sometimes I am thankful for all these trips because they end up teaching me lessons that shall stay with me for the rest of my life. Here, I will share one such incident as it really shaped my perspective.

Rameshwaram, considered to be one of the holiest lands in India, is home to innumerable pilgrimages as people from different parts of the country come here to seek blessings of God. There is a mythological story tied to the place. Like the rest of our countrymen, we too went to this place.

We did our chores and went to the temple and offered our prayers. If you have ever been to India, you would know that homelessness is an extremely common problem. You will find countless beggars loitering on the streets begging for alms and usually, people remain ignorant of such people because you really cannot give to all of them.

However, I distinctly recall one old lady who was sitting just outside the grand temple of Rameshwaram and she wasn't the kind of person who you could ignore. You could see her veins oozing from her skin and if skeletons were alive, I swear she resembled one.

Her eyes sat extremely low in their sockets and her lips were scaly dry. She approached us when we were clicking pictures and begged for money. My parents took one look at her and instantly they saw the frailness that pricked my heart, too. She was merely begging for five rupees that wouldn't even get her an entire loaf of bread, but don't we all say how God has a way of working up miracles?

In that instant of time, my father took pity on the unknown woman's sad state of affairs.

We were spending an excess of four grand every day staying at fancy hotels, buying homemade chocolates, and eating pizza topped with extra cheese and here she was – an old woman with perhaps no family to call her own, asking for five rupees so that she could have a morsel of food.

My parents asked her to accompany them to the nearest restaurant and she was too stunned to speak. She didn't say a word and I followed them out of curiosity. When we reached the restaurant, my parents asked her to sit down and gave her the menu card.

My dad told her, "Order whatever you want."

She gave an extremely surprised look and pushed the menu card and murmured something in Tamil, their native language. My parents couldn't understand what she was saying and the server translated for us.

"I can't read... I haven't eaten in thirteen days. I will have anything which is priced the lowest. Maybe, tea will do too."

I almost broke down on hearing this. The pain, agony, and pathos – it was unbearable. I have taken too much in my life for granted. Thirteen days without a meal. No wonder she looked frail. My dad then ordered a complete meal for her with a big dosa, the favorite Tamil food, along with sambar vada and a Coke as well. She had never tasted anything like Coke in her whole life and she gobbled up the entire dish in less than ten minutes.

The expression on her face was priceless. It wasn't the costliest restaurant and the bill was less than 400 INR. My mother asked if she needed anything else and at that instant, she fell on her feet. My mother jumped back and asked her not to do so, but tears were flowing down her cheeks and she sobbed and said,

"You're God's incarnation... let me touch your feet. My life shall get a meaning. I have waited thirteen days without food, but if I knew it was leading me to you, God's incarnation; I would wait another thirteen days."

My parents were a little embarrassed because after all, they're humans and not God. They tried to explain it to her, but what she said later was a lesson so important that I am going to take it to my grave.

"God isn't just an idol. I have never been to school, but I have spent my whole life begging outside one of the holiest temples in India. God resides in each one of us and He comes in various forms. You may have committed a hundred sins, but nothing you did harmed me. However, for me, you're the God who came in form of a blessing. I would have died in another couple of days, but you gave me my life. For me, you both will always be God. Just like I have found mine, you will also find yours. Make sure to thank the Lord when he comes because God is not just an idol. God resides in each one of us."

I stood there, comprehending the depth of what had just been told. Yes, indeed God is nothing if not the spirit who bestows us with love. He comes in various forms and we often fail to marvel at His magnificence. That little lunch with a random old woman taught me more than what the entire trip had taught me. My parents spotted me standing near the door with tears strumming down my cheeks and called me near. The old lady looked at me, smiled and blessed the three of us before she parted ways.

Her words rang in my ears many times and stayed with me, not just for the trip, but even today. Sometimes, we don't understand the magnanimity of our deeds. While it was just 400 INR for us, that little bit of money helped save someone's life and her lessons, in turn, molded mine.

I learned never to flinch from helping someone.

About the Author:

A misfit software engineer, Shruti Fatehpuria left work in the corporate world to pursue her dream. Her passion lies in talking of things she relates with and living the stories she often dreams of. Born in India, Shruti grew up with too many fairy tales and fancies living a life that turns out to be a story that can inspire others. She is on a voyage where she is in pursuit of herself and is sure that reality and her dreams will one day collide.

Figure 25. Outside the Temple that changed everything

Washing Clothes
By Guey J., China

I remember China as a very beautiful place, but one filled with painful memories. My childhood was like that of many survivors. We did what we could to make it through in those days. Unlike many, though, my family started fairly well off, having enjoyed meals to eat and a roof over our head. We had our own ancestrally-inherited compound, a vestige from the golden era when my great-grandfather advised for the Imperial Court, or so my family told me. We were very proud of our background back then. Our entire extended family lived together in houses intricately thatched together, as was customary, with our grand-aunt overseeing as the matriarch. She preferred keeping the family together and probably would have had her way if the war hadn't been so terrible.

The war started sometime before I was born, or at least, when I was too young to remember. My memory is hazy from the years that have gone by and sometimes because that is not a part of my life I like to think too much about. Everyone had their share of suffering. Food became scarce. People disappeared. But I know I am very lucky to have escaped multiple misfortunes through the kindness and help of strangers.

When I turned seventeen, my parents began to pressure me to marry. Given the political climate back then, there was talk of more war brewing. We had just come off of a long drawn-out battle with the Japanese. It was common knowledge that the *Gongchandang* and *Kuomingtang* had united briefly only to fight a common enemy, and those allegiances were shifting with the Japanese surrender. Undoubtedly, it was a dangerous time for young women to run around unescorted, especially those of the wrong class. If something should happen to us, then no one would want us anymore and we would be relegated to the trash. Not having an education, it would be difficult to find a job. It was just safer to marry us off as quickly as possible to as nice of a gentleman as could be found to help support us. That was the best that could be expected for young women back then.

My husband was a thirty-year-old soldier, who belonged to the *Kuomingtang* party. He had been introduced to the family as a friend and quickly accepted as an eligible bachelor. Our engagement was a whirlwind courtship, as we knew each other for only a short period of time before we married. Before turning eighteen, I found myself a bride and told to leave the house as I had a new home. Our union had started as a matter of convenience. However, I was luckier than many, because he treated me well.

Although my family had money, I did not inherit wealth. My husband received a small but generous dowry for my care, which we could have for building our future. But, in desperate times, many kinds of people are formed. A trustworthy contact of his, who would help us invest, turned out to be investing for riches of his own. We were swindled of literally everything but the clothes on our backs.

It was then that the *Gonchangdang* announced intentions to fight. With just our meager belongings, through help form a genuine friend of my husband's, we fled to the safety of Taiwan. It was only years later that I'd learn none of my family members who stayed in China (due to the paranoia of my grand-aunt, who feared losing her children), were ever heard from again. I can only hope that they started new lives, but the truth is that many probably died.

After we fled, life was hard again. We started off with nothing to our names. Having been raised in an upper-middle class family, I had not learned many of the skills that most girls my age would have, such as sewing or even waitressing. Embarrassingly, my reading skills were those of a third grader as I had stopped schooling early, which was common practice. *What need could women have for schooling?*

Many people, having struggles of their own, were indifferent to our plight. They had troubles themselves, such as feeding their own families. We survived through hard work, and learning as quickly as we could. A soldier's salary goes only so far for a family of two. Through the kindness of strangers who were willing to take a chance, I got a job in a factory.

I remember waiting in line to get water to wash our clothes at the public well.

Barely more than a teenager myself, I would rub my hands raw trying to get the dirt out of our garments. It would take me hours by the side of the sink to get the grime out. Tears streaming down my face, I thought only of the misery and troubles before us. How much I missed my family. How scary and foreign the world seemed. But, it was then, at my worst moment, that I met an angel. Her name was *Chen Shou Dong*, or "Winter" in Chinese, as her parents had named her after the winter season in which she had been born. She was the sweetest human I have ever known.

By the side of the tub, she patiently showed me how to wash clothes. You had to take the garments and scrub them on the sleeves and collars, where the dirt collects. You wash the armpits to take out the smell of the sweat and get rid of the stains. Somehow, learning how to clean clothes was a great step in what previously seemed an insurmountable task. I learned then that I could take care of myself with my own two hands, that things would be okay. Winter became a great friend of mine. Though over a half-century has passed since that day and though Winter has passed, I will always remember her kindness. I want to share it with the world. Small acts of kindness can have great impact and even last a lifetime, especially for those who need them most.

About the Author:
Guey J. was a wartime survivor of the Cultural Revolution in China. Her permanent residence is in southern Taiwan. She has three sons and seven grandchildren. She enjoys gardening and practicing Tai Chi with other grandparents.

What is Treasured on the Earth
By Hranush A., Armenia

I am a witness to the horrifying aftermath left by the Spitak earthquake, which took place in northern Armenia on December 7, 1988. The earthquake devastated my hometown, leaving buildings crumpled and people destitute. More than 25,000 people died in one day. My family, like thousands of others, was left without a home. Thousands of children were left without parents. Many millions, robbed of loved ones and possessions, were left with broken hearts. It was a huge disaster for us as a nation. Most people have probably forgotten these events because they happened so long ago, but those who lived through it never will. It was a trial that shaped us.

It was also one of my first memories. I was a three-year-old child who did not comprehend why there was so much blood. Blood was all over my friends from kindergarten, and bodies were everywhere. I did not understand why adults were carrying bodies into the streets. Only screams of people in the streets and the roar coming from the ruins gave me the sense that terrible things were happening in the world and no one was in control. As a child, I could never imagine death. I did not know death could be so close to us. It felt so scary and suddenly real.

We suffered privations and hardship. We were forced to become strong and grow up faster.

Before this earthquake, Gyumri, my town, had been rather prosperous, and the second largest city in the Soviet Republic of Armenia. We had led a carefree and easy way of life. We were a growing nation with peaceful enterprise and a rising economy. On that day, though, we lost our comfortable houses and untroubled lives. Death and disease took over. The survivors were forced to live in tin containers that barely resembled houses. There were none of the necessary conveniences: no toilet or running water, electricity, soap, etc. In those darkest moments, we learned many lessons: life could be unpredictable, random and cruel. We also found greatness in one other. We didn't lose our hope because all the world came together to help us.

Volunteers from Great Britain came to our town and brought assistance, including medical care, as well as blankets, beds, clothes, and other housekeeping goods. These rescuers were like angels from heaven in our moment of need. They lent us succor in our peril when all else was lost.

Although I didn't suffer physically directly due to the earthquake, I ended up breaking my right arm as I fell down from the upper berth of our tin container. In this chaos, a young doctor from the hospital nearby came to my aid. I distinctly remember he was a volunteer from the US.

Tall and muscular, I remember him looming above me with a concerned look on his face. He gingerly put my arm in a cast.

The day was cold, but he was heated from walking back and forth through the hospital from one ward to another, as many patients needed him. He repeatedly passed his handkerchief over his forehead, with a somewhat weary gesture, probably from the exhaustion of having to run from one emergency to the next. I looked at him as all the people in the hospital did, with admiration.

Sometime later, when the doctor removed my cast, he and my father had a conversation that I will never forget. My father asked him, "Why have you come to such a rotten place?" "Nothing of the kind," he answered. "A good name is better than riches." His words stayed with me. Even at three, I knew then that what he had said was true as I rubbed my broken arm. I remember how much it meant to be helped in an hour of need. It was more valuable than anything or any possession.

Twenty-six years have passed since those events, and Armenia has not yet fully recovered from the tragic consequences. However, the good deeds and kindness of people that we felt and experienced in those days had great impacts on our lives. I am proud to announce that the great admiration and respect for that doctor made me become a surgeon, as I grew up with the desire to help people as he had.

People like those volunteers helped us rise from our ashes. My deepest respect and thanks I extend to all of them, from the bottom of my heart. I want to conclude with this saying: "Virtue and kindness ennoble the man." A kind deed is never forgotten. It is a gesture that may change the course of a life.

About the Author:

Hranush A. is a young representative of the Armenian nation. She studied English at the American University of Armenia and medicine at Yerevan State Medical University. She is a children's surgeon as well as a writer. She enjoys both of her professions and tries to do her best at each one.

What Kindness Is
By H. R. Chang, Taiwan

When I was a little girl, our family was quite poor. I wouldn't have known that, though, because I was a pretty happy child, except the day the two neighborhood girls told me about my "condition." I remember learning what mean was on the same day that I learned what kindness was.

"Hsiu, what's wrong with you?" the two sisters shouted as they ran towards me.

I blinked. Even at four, I sensed that this was a pointed question. Approaching closer, I could see the sneers on their faces.

The two older girls stared angrily at me, evidently riled further by my lack of immediate reaction.

"Why are your clothes so tattered?" they demanded.

I was sure no answer would've really satisfied them.

"It's because you are POOR," one shouted, as the other pushed me to the ground.

I remember how hard the dirt floor was. I remember how high the soft yellow-brown dust kicked up into the air, and the iron taste of it in my dry mouth. The pain of my fall was mixed with confusion at how horrible being poor must be, if it could cause so much offense. Although I wish to say that I, like a heroine, got right back up, I remember crying loudly instead.

At that moment, a neighborhood lady came running across the street. Though I had never met her before, she rushed to my aid like a guardian angel flying to the rescue. Obaasan was a wartime widow who was actually Japanese. As a Hokkien Taiwanese, we hardly interacted with outsiders. The war had just recently ended. Occupation had brought foreigners to our home.

Obaasan demanded to know what the two young ladies thought they were doing and why they thought it was okay to bully a younger child. They did not have a good answer for her. The same stupefied silence I had given them was what they gave back to Obaasan. Their eyes narrowed, but lowered in shame.

Obaasan gave them a lesson on what it meant to be a proper lady before finally shooing the sulking girls away. The pair never bothered me again. I made a genuine friendship then – it was the beginning of something great.

Although we lived in the same neighborhood, I learned people can be kind, or not. My family received clothes from the Catholic church in our town. New clothes were too expensive. There was nothing "wrong" with us. Donated clothes were practical for an honest working family. The war had scattered a lot of people and made it hard to earn a living, as the economies were still ramping up. With two older brothers, it was hard for our family to spend cash on transient frivolities, such as replaceable fabric. There were more important things to consider, such as food and education.

Everyone once in a while, my family would be hungry and there wouldn't be enough for us. My mother would make us small bowls each. We would all get to eat and somehow she always claimed to be full, though I don't remember seeing her eat at all. My father was a farmer and a salesman, so he needed nutrition because he helped make money for our family with his two jobs. My brothers were rambunctious and need nutrition as growing boys. I was the only girl.

Although not rich herself, Obaasan was a widow who had a small pension and money saved. Comforting me, she took me inside her house to prepare some soup. She taught me the song, *Momotarō,* or "Peach Boy." Though being beaten up as a child is not exactly a memory I cherish, I am happy that it led me to meeting the wonderful elder lady, Obaasan.

I learned what kind and cruel are that day. I learned the kindness of strangers can rescue you at a moment when you least expect it. It can lead to lifelong friendships. It can make your worst memories a ray of sunshine. Thank you, Obaasan. You taught me that good is definitely greater than evil.

About the Author:

H. R. enjoys playing the piano and going for walks in nature. She has become a successful career woman but never forgets her roots.

Yissus' Smile

By Prusevie Boncato-Bekalo, Ethiopia

When he smiled, his white teeth gleamed brightly through the cleft in his lip. A slight, scrawny boy with tattered, worn-thin shorts, he danced eagerly from one bare foot to another, awaiting his next task. His English was pieced and broken but he sounded out the words he did know carefully and painstakingly. The missionaries had noticed him immediately – partly because of the gaping split in his lip that started just below his left nostril, but mostly because of his intense desire to learn – it emanated from his earth-toned body in almost palpable waves. The Palms, a Caucasian missionary couple, had found the small village of Abonsa through their Adventist outreach and settled in a small mission outpost. The compound had a church, a primary school, and a clinic that served the rural Ethiopian community in that area. The compound was always teeming with young and old from near and far. Sick people from surrounding villages traveled miles on foot or donkey to benefit from the *ferenji* medicine. (*Ferenji* is an Ethiopian term for foreigner, a corrupted version of "French.")

The Palms had an old, battered car that would send the children tumbling over one another in fear whenever it jolted, sputtered or coughed in their direction. The children often crowded the church compound, their dusty bodies pressed tight against each other as they strained to watch the missionaries do their work, oohing and aahing at their strange ways. The young boy would recall years later the first time he saw an automobile while walking through the brush. A large metal monster he had never seen before came bearing down on him at breakneck speed. The driver, perhaps out of warning, or more likely out of malicious humor, upped the ante and let out piercing blasts of the car horn, hurling the young boy into the bushes in a panic.

Isaac, for that was his name, stood apart from the others, even in the hordes of wiggling, excitable children that flocked to the church compound. This was not only because of his disfigurement, although it did make him an easy target for teasing and ridicule from the other children. He didn't hang back in shyness, or wander away once his curiosity was satisfied. Instead, he watched intently, learning new words, jumping in to run errands for the missionaries, no matter how small the task. They would find him in the church compound whenever he wasn't taking the cows to the river or tending to the farm with his brothers, bursting with energy and excitement despite the five-kilometer trek to school and back.

Most boys would take advantage of the short hours they had to spare between herding cows, tending the fields and going to school by playing or just goofing about. Isaac instead would gladly crouch down in the dirt with the missionary wives, helping them tend to their garden and amazing them with his agricultural knowledge. He would volunteer to babysit the missionary children while their parents worked in the clinic or church. But most of all, Isaac loved to learn. His eyes shining with intelligence, he quickly picked up and put into practice new words he heard the missionaries speak. He quickly became a translator for the missionaries, speaking and interpreting for his neighbors.

The Palms would see Isaac in the early morning light running with his books, sure-footed on the beaten, rock-riddled path to the small schoolhouse. He loved school – his mother would recall with sad fondness how he came home weeping bitterly the first day of enrollment. The teachers had not allowed him into the first grade because of his diminutive stature and his inability to meet the prerequisite of the time – reaching over his head with his right hand to touch the tip of his left ear.

He had to wait for another year before being allowed into the schoolhouse. He would listen to their chanting of the Ethiopian alphabet as he pressed his face to the rickety wooden fence surrounding the school compound, silently imitating their melodic, sing-song repetitions.

He spent the long year before the next admitting term stretching his little arms as high up as he could and reaching desperately for his ear. He would not be refused admission again! At last, when he was finally admitted to school, he would wait eagerly for his turn to hold the eucalyptus stick and point out the Amharic characters on a chart fixed high up on the mud wall.

His mother always silently blamed herself for Yissu's (for that is what she affectionately called him) year off from school. He had always been a sickly child – his birth defect, though slight and only mildly disfiguring, made breastfeeding difficult for the infant, and infections commonplace when he was a toddler. While still pregnant with him, her second-to-last-born child of eight, a man had paid her husband (a respected village elder) a visit. As the men sat around the fire and she prepared the evening meal, she had caught a glimpse of him in the firelight and seen the awful split in his lip. The guest struggled to blow on some embers of the evening fire, for it was a chilly night, but his puffs of air escaped through his harelip and produced little effect. She had waited until she was safely out of earshot before she burst into helpless laughter. She would deeply regret her discreet mirth months later when her son was born with the same affliction.

Though scientifically, Yissu's harelip could be explained as a genetic mishap or nutritional deficiency, in that Ethiopian culture it is widely, superstitiously believed that birth defects and illnesses that befall children are a result of or tied to parental behavior. She even named him Isaac, meaning "laughter" in the Bible, a reminder of what she believed was punishment for her mocking.

It wasn't long before the missionaries began to look forward to seeing Isaac standing in the compound, smiling brightly through his harelip. Soon they began to depend on him to translate at the clinic, sought his sage eleven-year-old advice when it came to their garden vegetables. Their children would ask after him, playfully grabbing at his face and tugging at his thick kinky hair when he would settle down to play with them in the dirt.

Perhaps secretly he cherished their child-like innocence and acceptance of him, despite his disfigurement. The Palms began to prayerfully ponder; how could they repay this boy for all he did for them? They finally broached an idea – would he like to have the harelip fixed?

Fixed? He had never thought it possible. What did it even mean to be fixed? The missionaries tried to explain. They would take him to the Adventist hospital in Addis Ababa, the capital city, where they would close his lip, and he would look like everyone else. He ran home to tell his family; his mother's breath caught in her throat, half-fearful, half-hopeful. His father, strong and stern, shook his head; they simply couldn't afford the white man's medicine. Suddenly, his oldest brother Tesfaye, a newlywed and active member in the church, stepped forward. He would sell one of his yearling calves for the procedure. He had always had a soft spot in his heart for Isaac, hurt internally each time the other children poked fun at his face. While he had chased off the children, chided them for their hurtful remarks, more would come, and he could not always be there. He would help. If it meant not having to see the unshed tears gleam in his brother's eyes when others saw his face and shunned him, he would pay for the *ferenji's* medicine.

Isaac was ecstatic. His lip would be fixed! He would go on a trip, to the capital! He had never been farther than the surrounding towns where his father would preach, running alongside his father's mule for miles when he was allowed to tag along. And this time he would be in a car! The Palms quickly arranged for the long ride to the capital. On the day of travel, they presented Isaac with an incredible gift; a pair of bright red trousers two sizes too large, his very first pair of long pants. The pants had been pulled out of the "missionary box" – clothing sent all the way to Yissu's village by well-wishers overseas. The trousers barely hung onto his waist, but Yissu hitched them high, a lip-splitting smile spread wide on his ebony face. His deft hands quickly improvised a belt made of braided ensete (false banana) fiber – and he strutted around with the baggy pants, drawing furious envy from his younger brother, who coveted his upcoming trip and the long pants.

On the day of travel, Isaac had awoken earlier than usual, hours before the sun, and took the cattle down to the river one more time. He gathered his precious bundle of threadbare clothes and food his mother wrapped in banana leaves and stepped nervously into the Palms' car for the first time. He waved to his mother, standing outside of their square mud hut, until she was completely out of sight, and shouted and laughed at his brothers and friends who ran alongside the car until they could no longer keep up.

The car ride was hours long and very bumpy. The whole stretch to Addis Ababa was all-weather rough road. Asphalt streets had not reached his province yet; it was still only the 1960s. Isaac kept his face plastered to the window, taking in the sights and sounds of a whole new world. He had never seen buildings so tall. And so many, many cars.

They arrived at the Adventist hospital in the late evening. It was called Zewditu Hospital, after an Ethiopian empress. The hospital was so clean and white, the bed sheets so crisp and cool. Isaac was settled into his hospital room, and after assurances that they would come see him first thing in the morning, the Palms left to sleep at the Adventist guest house. The next morning, they found Yissu sleeping on the floor next to his hospital bed – he had never slept on a raised bed before. Each turn of his body had made terrifying squeaking noises emanate from the bed, and he was convinced it would crumble underneath him.

The nurses and *ferenji* doctors were all very friendly and kind. The surgeon came into the room and met Isaac. Immediately recognizing the intelligence of his young patient, the surgeon explained the procedure. They would sew his lip shut – it wouldn't look better the first few days, and might even hurt, but eventually there would be nothing there but a faint scar. Isaac nodded in quiet understanding; he had begun to long for his mother and the familiarity of home. The nurses assisted him with a bath before the surgery, and the crystal clear water flowing like rain from the sparkling shower head onto the white marble tub surface bewildered him. The missionaries gathered around his bed right before the surgery and bowed their heads, praying for a successful surgery for this boy they had come to cherish and love.

When Isaac awoke hours later, he saw through the fog of the fading anesthesia the friendly *ferenji* surgeon and the smiling Palms. The surgeon came close and held up a mirror - Isaac could not believe his eyes. He looked so different! He faintly heard the surgeon talk about swelling and his face going back to normal size in a few days, but he could barely pay attention. He gingerly touched his upper lip, and felt all warm and glowing inside. He looked new! He looked like the other children!

The Palms stayed for two weeks at the church headquarters in Addis Ababa, and by the time they were ready to return to their mission outpost, Isaac had fully recuperated. The Palm's old trusty car had barely creaked to a stop in front of Isaac's home before he bolted out the door and ran to his family, running from member to member showing off his new lip, causing a great commotion. His mother held him tight to her chest, her worry and guilt melting away. His father held his son's face between his large, calloused hands and smiled. The whole village marveled at the *ferenji's* medicine – the missionaries had fixed what many had thought was a life-long affliction.

The kindness of the Palms had a lasting impact on young Isaac. He continued to dedicate his time and energy at the church compound, and their consideration impressed on him a need to pass on a similar kindness whenever he had the opportunity.

He continued on to high school, where he met and began to work with a veteran missionary lady, Gladys Martin, who dedicated forty years of her life to the Ethiopian people. She taught him how to drive a big long-body Toyota Land Cruiser. He became her assistant, going deep into the rural bush to immunize thousands of children. He would help her load several women who suffered from birthing complications into the Land Cruiser and transport them to the Fistula Hospital in Addis Ababa.

Each trip to the capital would remind him of that very first car ride, as a fearful but excited lad of thirteen with the bunny lip. Miss Martin encouraged Isaac to pursue university studies in the newly-established University of Eastern Africa in Kenya, where he became part of the first graduating class in 1983. He then went on to the Philippines for masters and doctoral studies, where he met his wife and started his family.

Isaac, the young, sickly child from a small village in Ethiopia, never forgot the kindness of the missionaries. He spent his life paying it back and paying it forward, and continues to do so today. He sponsored three of his older brother Tesfaye's children and sent them to school overseas, the same older brother who sacrificed his precious cattle for Isaac's life-changing surgery. In 1992, he sent a ticket to Miss Martin, who had retired to California, to visit his young family in the Philippines. Isaac is currently the president of a non-profit organization that helps rural communities, advocating for gender equality and providing schools for children who do not have access. He and his wife founded a school in southern Ethiopia a few hours away from his home village: a school that provides education to thousands of children from kindergarten all the way through high school.

If you ask him now whether his success is closely and irrevocably linked to the kindness that missionaries showed him, a lip-splitting smile will break over his kind, weathered face, and he will say "Yes."

About the Author:

Prusevie Boncato-Bekalo is happily married to Isaac. Nairobi, Kenya, has been home to the Bekalos since mid-1994. Prusevie is a teacher and currently designs complementary/supplemental curricula and instructional materials for the family-owned K-12 BNB Learning Centre in Awassa, southern Ethiopia. Isaac and Prusevie have two grown daughters who are pursuing their careers in the US.

Acknowledgements

I would like to thank my family and friends for their support, and the wonderful writers who contributed to this compilation. Without you all, this book wouldn't have been possible.

Additional Information

For more information on Reading Harbor Publications, we invite you to visit our website at www.readingharbor.com.

For interaction with other fans of "Seeking Human Kindness", please visit www.seekinghumankindness.com.

"Be a rainbow in someone else's cloud." ~ Maya Angelou

Made in the USA
San Bernardino, CA
29 September 2014